THE REAL BOOK OF SCIENCE

EXPERIMENTS

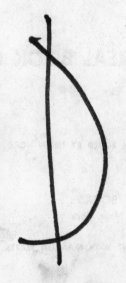

THE REAL BOOK OF

EDITED BY HELEN HOKE

GARDEN CITY BOOKS
Garden City, New York

BY ARRANGEMENT WITH FRANKLIN WATTS, INC.

SCIENCE
EXPERIMENTS

BY JOSEPH LEEMING

Illustrated by Bette J. Davis

1862

507.2
Lee
1968 / NDEA
Painter School

With deep gratitude to Ned Lehac, teacher of science at the Thomas Knowlton Junior High School in New York City, for his helpful suggestions concerning the manuscript of this book.

Contents

A WORD TO BEGINNING SCIENTISTS

Do YOU WANT to find out exciting facts about the physical world? If you do, the best way to go about it is to do your own science experiments.

Scientists have found out *how* natural forces act, and *why* they act the way they do, by experimenting. They have learned how air, water, electricity, heat, cold, light and sound and other natural forces work. By doing the experiments in this book you can demonstrate these things for yourself, right in your own home.

Most people are apt to think of a scientific experiment as something that has to be done in a big laboratory where solemn men in white uniforms work with test tubes and other special equipment. That just isn't true at all! There are hundreds of fascinating experiments that you can do easily with common materials found in almost every kitchen. Glasses and bottles can be your test tubes and beakers. Balloons, paper bags, and teakettles can serve as your scientific equipment.

You don't need any knowledge of science to do these experiments. All you need is curiosity! But as you go along you will learn quite a bit about science that you didn't know before. You can amaze your friends, too (and perhaps even some of your teachers), with these intriguing, easy-to-do experiments. Best of all, you'll find that you have a wonderful time doing them.

Joseph Leeming

THE REAL BOOK OF SCIENCE EXPERIMENTS

AIR IS AMAZING

HARDLY ANYONE pays much attention to the air. It is invisible, and we never feel it unless a strong wind rushes along, blowing things before it. But even though we are rarely conscious of it, the air is always around us. It is an amazing and very powerful substance, with characteristics that few people know anything about.

We live in a world that is always in motion. Even still air and ice and solid rock are filled with movement. This movement is the dancing of the tiny molecules that make up all matter. (A molecule is the smallest possible unit of a compound.) The molecules, in turn, are made up of still tinier atoms, which are the smallest units of elements.

In air, which is a mixture of gases, this dance takes the form of a fast free-for-all, in which the individual molecules move at speeds of nearly 250 miles an hour and bump into other molecules five thousand million times a second. Our skin receives the impact of these countless tiny "bullets," and it registers on our bodies as air pressure. Usually we don't feel this pressure because it is equaled by pressure from inside our bodies.

Air pressure is so great that air is sometimes called an "invisible giant." Right this minute your body is supporting fourteen tons of air pressure. That is the weight of the air that is pressing against you.

The weight of small quantities of air is, of course, very slight. But when you realize that every square foot of the earth's surface supports a column of air over two hundred miles high, which exerts a pressure of almost a ton on each square foot of surface, you can see that the weight of this much air mounts up.

Air is a mixture of 21 per cent oxygen and 78 per

cent nitrogen. The other 1 per cent consists of rare gases called argon, neon, krypton, etc.

Another interesting thing about air is that it contains at all times large quantities of water vapor. We can rarely see this water, but it is there just the same, like a huge invisible ocean over our heads.

In the following experiments you can demonstrate how powerful air pressure really is, you can weigh air, compress it, pour it, and make it obey your commands in several other ways.

STEEL WOOL

How to Take Oxygen Out of the Air

It may hardly seem possible that, in your own home and without expensive laboratory equipment, you can draw oxygen right out of the air. Yet it is one of the easiest experiments in this whole book!

All you need is a drinking glass, a soup plate, and

a little steel wool. (This is used for cleaning pots and pans, and you can get it at the ten-cent store if there is none in the house.)

Tear off enough steel wool to cover the bottom of the glass. Run some hot water into the kitchen sink and put a cake of soap in the water. Let the soap dissolve until you have a good soapy solution. Wash the steel wool in this solution in order to get rid of any protective oily covering there may be on it.

When the steel wool has dried, wedge it tightly in the bottom of the glass. Then fill a soup plate with water. Turn the glass upside down and stand it on the plate.

The oxygen in the air will be attracted to the iron in the steel wool, and soon will start rusting it. As this goes on, the steel wool will absorb more and more of the oxygen, and the water will be pushed up into the glass by outside air pressure to fill the space previously occupied by the oxygen. Within a few hours the process will be completed. Almost all of the oxygen will be drawn out of the air, and the one-fifth part of the glass that it formerly occupied will be filled with water.

NEWSPAPER

SLAT OF WOOD

How to Prove the Strength of Air Pressure

Here is a very easy and dramatic way to prove how great air pressure is.

Get a very thin piece of wood about three feet long and four inches wide. (A thin slat from a fruit crate is good.) Lay the slat on a table so that one end sticks out about four inches beyond the table edge. Then put two double sheets of newspaper over the part of the wood that is on the table. Put the papers one on top of the other and smooth them down with your hand, pressing them close against the slat and the table.

Now strike the end of the slat a hard downward blow with your closed fist or, better still, with a baseball bat. You might expect this to throw the paper into the air. But the air says, "No, you don't. I'm heavy enough to stop any nonsense like that." It presses down so hard on the paper that the slat breaks beneath your blow!

It is hard to believe that air has as much pressure as this. But if you figure it out, remembering that air exerts a pressure of almost one ton on every square foot of surface, you will see that it exerts a pressure of more than five tons on an outspread double sheet of newspaper. It is almost as if five tons of bricks were piled up on top of the paper.

How to Make Water Compress Air

If you blow up a balloon to a good size, and then decide to blow it up a little fuller, you can do so. The balloon will expand a little, and at the same time you will pack in the air more tightly. You can compress air so as to fit more of it into a given space.

But water is different. When you fill a glass to the brim with water, the glass is full. You just can't compress the water in order to put more of it into the glass.

With a tall drinking glass and a straight-sided medicine vial you can show how air compresses and water doesn't. If there is no vial of this kind in the house, you can get one for a few cents at the drugstore.

First fill the glass almost to the brim with water. Then fill the vial about half full. Turn the vial up-

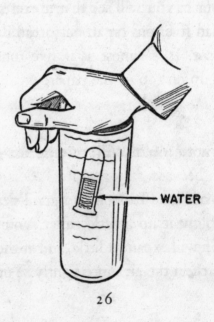

WATER

side down and float it in the glass. You will probably have to try a few times before you get just the right amount of water in the vial. It should just barely float.

Now cover the rim of the glass completely with the palm of your right hand. Press your palm down hard and a little way into the glass. This pressure on the water will force water up into the vial. The new water will compress the air in the vial. The vial will be heavier because it contains more water. As a result, it will sink down toward the bottom of the glass.

Raise your hand and the vial will rise as the compressed air in it forces out some of the water.

How to Make Air Pressure Crush a Tin Can

You do not feel the great pressure of air against your body because the pressure inside your body equals that outside. If you didn't have this air inside your body, the outside air pressure would squash you flat. The same is true of a house. If you could remove all the air from inside a house, the outside air pressure of many hundreds of tons would instantly crush it like an eggshell.

You can demonstrate this enormous crushing power of the air very easily by using an empty straight-sided one-gallon can with a screw-on cap, plus the kitchen stove. Paints and varnishes come in cans of the kind needed. If you don't have one, you can probably get an empty one at a hardware store.

To start the experiment remove the screw cap and pour half a cup of water into the can. Put the can on the stove and bring the water to a boil. (This will fill the can with steam, which forces out all the air. But the pressure of the steam inside the can will balance the pressure of the air outside.) Let the

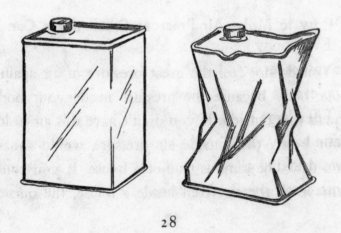

water boil for several minutes. Then lift the can from the stove and put it in a pan on the table. As soon as the amount of steam coming out of the top of the can lessens enough to permit, screw on the cap tightly.

Now pour some cold water over the can to hasten its cooling off. This is what happens: The steam cools and changes to water. The can is then no longer completely filled with anything—water, steam, or air. Instead, there is a partial vacuum inside it. The substances inside the can are not strong enough to equal the force of the outside air pushing against the sides of the can. Soon, with loud moans and groans, the outside air crushes in the sides of the can.

How to "Pour" Air

Everybody knows that you can pour water or milk or any other liquid. But very few people realize that you can, so to speak, pour air, too!

Fill a large basin with water or, if you have no big basin handy, fill the kitchen sink or a washbasin. Put two drinking glasses within easy reach. Fill one glass with water by dipping it into the basin. Turn it upside down and set it down that way without losing any of the water.

Turn the second glass upside down and hold it in the basin without letting it touch the bottom. It is full of air. You will see that no water comes up into it because the air is a real substance and occupies all the space in the glass.

The next step is to pour the air from this glass into the first glass. Move the second glass close to the first one. Then tip it a little and move its mouth under the mouth of the first glass. Lift up the first glass to make this possible.

As you tip the glass the air inside it will bubble out and will rise up into the other glass, forcing the water out. At the same time water will flow into the glass that was filled with air. You are "pouring" air from one glass into the other.

Actually, the air is squeezed into the glass by the greater weight and pressure of the surrounding water, very much as a slippery watermelon seed can be squeezed and made to fly off into space by the pressure of your thumb and forefinger. Because air cannot be dissolved in water and is much lighter than water it is very easily pushed upward by the water.

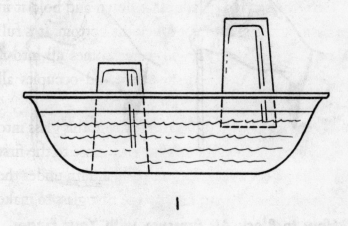

I

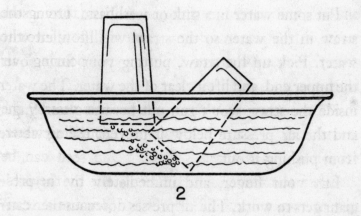

2

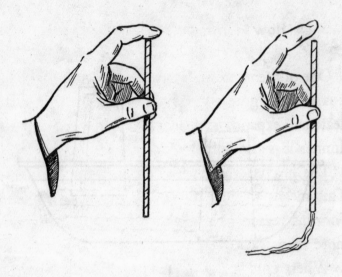

How to Block Air Pressure with Your Finger

Put some water in a sink or washbasin. Lay a soda straw in the water so the straw will be filled with water. Pick up the straw, putting your finger over the upper end, and lift it clear of the water. The water inside the straw won't run out because your finger and the air pressure below it prevent the air above from pushing it out.

Lift your finger, and immediately the invisible giant gets to work. The air presses down on the water and forces it out of the straw, overcoming the upward pressure of the air beneath.

How to Trace Warm Air Currents

One of the interesting things about air is that when it is warm it goes up away from the earth. As air is heated it expands and becomes thinner. Since it is thinner it is also lighter than cold air.

The heavier cold air is "denser" than warm air. This means that its molecules are closer together. For this reason it is drawn downward by gravity more than warm air is.

When cold air is pulled toward the earth by gravity, it pushes away the warm air that is near the floor or the earth. We say that warm air "rises," but it is really pushed up by the dense cold air that flows down and takes its place.

A good way to demonstrate how warm air rises is shown in this experiment. Put a lighted candle on the ground between two pieces of wood or two flat stones. Then put a cardboard mailing tube over the candle. This will fill the tube with warm air.

Now roll up a paper napkin or a paper towel; touch a lighted match to one end and then quickly blow out the flame. This will make the paper smoke. Pick up the tube and hold the smoking end of the paper near the bottom of the tube. The warm air in the tube, which is rising, will draw the smoke up with it.

The hot sun creates many columns of heated air that move upward in this way, and aviators are very familiar with them. They call them "thermals," from the Greek word *thermos*, meaning "hot." These currents, rushing up from the ground, often toss airplanes around as though they were leaves or pieces of paper.

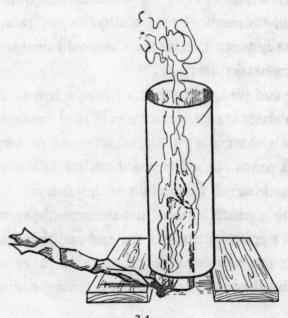

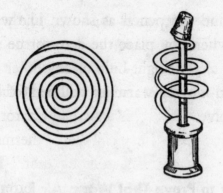

A Warm-Air-Current Detector

If you make a warm-air-current detector like the one shown in the diagram, you can locate thermals in many places, both indoors and outdoors.

The detector is made from a circle of paper about five inches in diameter. Draw a spiral line on the paper and cut along it with a pair of scissors. Leave a circle about the size of a quarter in the center.

Put a thimble on the center and draw around it with a pencil. Then, using a sharp-pointed knife, cut this circle out of the center.

Push a pencil into a spool and put a pin into the pencil's eraser. Then put the thimble on top of the pin. It can revolve easily because there is very little friction between it and the pin. Put the spiral of paper around the pencil as shown in the diagram.

Now, when you place the detector on a radiator or over an electric light bulb or any other hot place, the upward-moving warm air will make the spiral of paper revolve.

How to Prove That Warm Air Expands

It is easy enough to say that warm air expands. But if someone says, "I don't believe it. You've got to prove it to me!" how could you meet his challenge? A scientist must be able to prove that the things he says are true. This experiment proves dramatically that air expands when it is heated.

To do the experiment you will need a soda-pop bottle, a balloon, and a saucepan. Squeeze the air out of the balloon and then fit the mouth of the balloon over the top of the bottle. Put the bottle in the sauce-pan and fill the pan half full of cold water. Then heat the water by putting the pan on the stove.

As the water heats it will warm the air inside the bottle. The air will expand. Needing more space, it will rise and blow up the balloon.

36

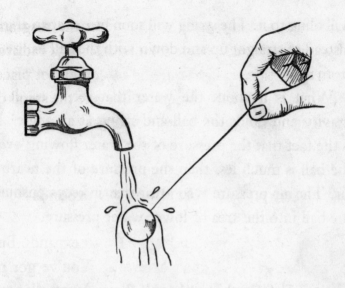

How to Make Air Pressure Overcome Gravity

This experiment sounds impossible—but try it!

All you need is a ping-pong ball fastened with tape to one end of a piece of string about a foot long. Take the ball to a sink or washbasin, turn on the cold-water tap, and hold the ball in the stream of water. Then slowly move the string to one side, away from the water.

You would expect the string to draw the ball with it and leave the stream of water. But some mysterious force is at work. Instead of leaving the water, the ball will cling to it. The string will soon be out at an angle instead of straight up and down with the ball hanging from it.

What is it about the water that seems to defy gravity and holds the ball and string at an angle? It is the fact that the pressure of the water flowing over the ball is much less than the pressure of the nearby air. The air pressure is so great that it keeps pushing the ball into the area of lower water pressure.

The Card That Won't Blow Away

This is another surprising experiment that shows the power of air pressure.

Get a spool, a small square of cardboard, and a pin. Stick the pin halfway through the center of the cardboard. Then hold the cardboard against one end of the spool so the pin fits in the center opening of the spool, and blow smoothly and steadily into the other end. Instead of being blown away, the cardboard will stick fast to the spool as though it were glued in place!

The explanation is that the swiftly moving air you blow through the spool and against the card exerts less pressure against the card than does the undisturbed air on the opposite side. The moving air, trying to escape at the sides of the card, doesn't push as hard against the card as the still air does.

This creates a small area of low pressure between the spool and the card. The air on the opposite side of the card immediately tries to fill up this low-pressure area and, in doing so, forces the card against the spool.

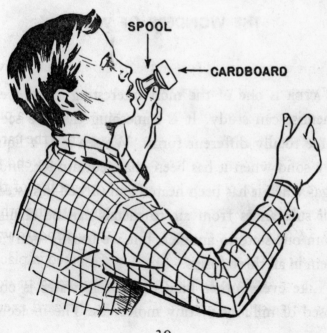

SPOOL

CARDBOARD

THE WONDERS OF WATER

WATER is one of the most interesting substances a scientist can study. It is something that we see in three totally different forms. We see it as a liquid, as a solid when it has been changed into ice, and as a gas when it has been heated and turned into steam. All substances from air to metals can be changed from one state to another, but we usually don't see them in all three forms.

Like every other kind of matter, water is composed of millions of tiny molecules. The molecules in water do not dance about as fast as they do in air. Instead, they slip past each other at slower speeds and the dance is more of a glide. When you heat water, however, the molecules speed up and jump around excitedly in every direction.

In the following experiments you will be able to expand water, make it lighter in weight, make it denser and heavier, and demonstrate other facts about it which you may not have known before.

How to Show That Heat Makes Water Lighter

To do this experiment you will need a drinking glass, a small pill bottle, and a fountain pen containing ink.

Fill the drinking glass nearly full of cold water; then pour cold water into the pill bottle until it is about two-thirds full. Put the point of the fountain pen into the bottle and push the plunger on the pen in order to force a few drops of ink into the water. Put the bottle right side up in the glass. Because the water in the bottle is cold, nothing will happen. The ink-colored water will stay in the bottle.

Now empty the bottle and refill it two-thirds full of hot water. Put a few drops of ink in it, as before, and set the bottle in the glass. At once an inky stream will start to rise up from the bottle. Because the water is hot, it is lighter and has less density than the cold water in the glass. When the inky water cools, it will become heavy again and will sink toward the bottom of the glass.

How to Increase the Density of Water

If you put an egg into an eight-ounce glass of water, it will immediately sink to the bottom. This is because the egg is denser than the water. Since it is denser, it weighs more than does an equal volume of water. A piece of any common wood, however, will float in water because it is less dense. It is lighter than an equal volume of water.

You can make an egg float in water by increasing the density of the water. Simply add two heaping tablespoonfuls of salt to the glass of water and stir with a spoon until the salt is dissolved. The salt will increase the water's density so that a given amount of the salt water will weigh more than the same amount of pure water.

Put the egg in the water again and this time it will

float. The water now has greater density than the egg.

This experiment illustrates why it is so easy for people to float in the Great Salt Lake in Utah. The water of the Great Salt Lake is very dense because of the huge amount of salt dissolved in it.

How to Show That There Is Space between Water's Molecules

To do the experiment, fill a glass to the brim with water. Then take a table salt shaker full of salt and pour the salt very slowly into the water. As you do this, keep stirring the water constantly with a straw taken from a broom or a piece of thin wire.

You will probably be able to empty the entire contents of the salt shaker into the glass. There will be a small increase in the volume of the water, but it will be only a fraction of the combined volume of the salt and the water.

The explanation of this experiment is probably that there are empty spaces between the molecules of the water. These spaces, though invisible, are large enough to hold the molecules of the dissolved salt.

HOT WATER   **COLD WATER**

Hot- and Cold-Water Race Shows Molecular Action

You have seen that when water is heated it gets lighter and expands. Now you can show that something else happens too. This is that heat speeds up the activity of the molecules in the water.

You can demonstrate this by staging a race between hot and cold water. Get two small tin cans of the same size and shape. Make a small hole with the point of a sharp nail 'or a fruit-juice-can opener in the bottom of each can. Fill one can with ice water and the other one with hot water. Then put each can on top of a drinking glass and watch what happens.

The hot water will flow into its glass much faster

than the cold water. Simply by heating the water you have caused an important change in the actions of its millions of individual molecules.

In cold water the molecules move slowly and tend to cling closely to each other. But when you heat water, the heat stirs up the molecules and makes them hurry about. In their hurry, they stop clinging to each other and, instead, they slide rapidly over each other.

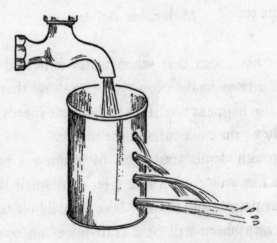

Water Pressure Increases with Depth

You don't have to put on a diver's suit and go down into the water to prove how quickly water pressure increases the deeper down you go. You can do it just by getting an empty tin can and punching four holes in it, one right under the other. (You can use an awl or even a nail.) Then hold the can under a faucet and turn on the water.

As soon as the can is full, streams of water will come out of all the holes. You will see that the two lower streams shoot out much farther than the two upper ones. This is because the water near the bottom of the can exerts much greater pressure than the water near the top.

How to Make Water Lift a Person

When you put flowers in water, the water pushes up through capillary tubes in the stems. ("Capillary" means "hairlike" or very small.) Many substances such as paper and cardboard have tubes of this kind, and water pushes into them in the same way as it flows into the capillary tubes of flower stems. This is known as "capillary action."

This experiment shows the great force exerted by water in capillary action. Get two tin cans of the same size and shape and cut off their tops smoothly. Then cut out a number of squares of porous cardboard or corrugated board. You should have enough squares to fill each can up to the level of the open top.

Ask a friend to stand on the cans, and then pour water into both cans. As the water pushes into the minute capillary tubes in the cardboard, it will make the cardboard swell so much that your friend will be lifted several inches into the air!

How to Boil Water with an Ice Cube

Scientists tell us that the boiling point of water changes according to the amount of air pressure on the water's surface. When the air pressure is increased, the water won't boil until it has been heated to a higher temperature than usual. When the air pressure is reduced, the water will boil at a lower temperature.

Here is an experiment that proves it. You will need the bottom part of a pyrex coffee maker, like the one shown in the drawing, and a cork with which to stopper it. A heatproof glass container is needed because an ordinary glass one might crack during the experiment.

Fill the container half an inch deep with water. Then put it on the stove and boil the water. This will fill the pot with steam and will drive out all the air.

Now take the pot from the stove and hold it in your hand. As soon as the steam dies down a little, put in the cork. Turn the pot upside down and put an ice cube on it or squeeze a spongeful of cold water over it. Immediately the water will start to boil again.

Why does the ice cube or cold water make the water boil?

The answer is that the cold lowers the pressure of the air above the water. It does this by changing the water vapor in the pot into a liquid. As the air pressure is suddenly reduced, the boiling point of the water is also reduced. The heat remaining in the water is then enough to make it boil.

How to Float Steel on Water

Everybody thinks that a piece of metal dropped into water will immediately sink to the bottom. But you can make a steel object which is much denser than water float on the surface of the water!

To do the experiment, fill a cup with water and then put a razor blade on the prongs of a fork. Lower the fork slowly and carefully into the water. When the razor blade rests on the water, it will float there.

This is possible because water has an invisible skin that is called "surface tension." This is caused by the

51

action of the molecules on the surface of the water. When they are in contact with air, they are attracted more strongly than usual to the water to which they belong. They do not want to join the air and are repelled by it. This packs them more tightly together and makes them form a strong surface layer of molecules on top of the water.

This layer is dense enough to support a razor blade or a steel needle. It is also strong enough to support flies and water insects, which can walk on top of the water.

How to Make Water's Surface Tension Propel a Boat

You can use the surface tension of water to propel a little boat around a pan of water at a good rate of speed. People who don't know their science will wonder what it is that makes the boat go.

Cut a piece of cardboard or very thin wood into the shape of a boat about an inch and a half long. With a knife make a V-shaped slit in the stern and wedge a small thin piece of soap into the slit. Then fill a pan with water and put the boat on the water. The boat will immediately start to move forward, just as though it were propelled by a motor.

The reason for the boat's motion is this: As the soap slowly dissolves, it lowers the surface tension of the water at the stern of the boat, making the tension just behind the boat lower than the tension in front of it. The boat will keep moving until the surface tension of all the water in the pan has been lowered by the soap.

How to Waterproof Your Skin

This experiment looks like magic, but it is based on a scientific principle. You can have a good time showing it to your friends. In front of them you fill a bowl with ordinary water. Then you dip your hand in the water and bring it out absolutely dry.

You do the trick by rubbing zinc stearate bath powder all over one hand, including the fingers. You can buy this powder at a drugstore. Use pressure when you are rubbing it on so that it will get into your skin. It is perfectly harmless. Then, when you put your hand in the water and take it out again quickly, your hand will remain dry.

The explanation is that water molecules are repelled by the zinc stearate. Ordinarily, when you put your hand in water it becomes wet because water molecules are attracted to your hand more strongly than they are to each other. But when zinc stearate is on your hand, the water molecules cling more closely together and stay in the water.

HAVE FUN WITH HEAT

THE HEAT with which all of us are most familiar is the warmth of the sun. But we also know of the heat given off by stoves, radiators, wood fires, and even candles. Heat is a very powerful and active force. It stirs up the molecules in everything it touches and makes them dance at a faster pace.

In addition to warming things, heat also makes many things grow larger or expand. When you heat water or other liquids, they expand. When the sun heats the mercury in a thermometer, it expands and pushes its way up the tube of the thermometer to show a higher temperature. In the same way, heat expands gases like air or steam. It is the expansion of steam that makes a steam engine go, and it is the expansion of heated air that drives an automobile engine.

Heat also expands metals. That is why there is always a space between the ends of the rails in a railroad track. It leaves room for the rails to expand in hot weather. Scientists have calculated that the difference in length between winter and summer of the rails of a stretch of track 500 miles long is about 1,400 feet, or a quarter of a mile!

Heat is a form of energy that travels through the air in waves. Heat waves and light waves are much the same except in length. Heat waves can be reflected and broken up just as can light waves.

Another scientific fact about heat is that it travels at different speeds through different substances. All substances conduct heat, but some conduct it so slowly that they are called insulators. Metals are usually good heat conductors while both air and water are poor conductors.

There is tremendous energy in heat. If you wanted

to heat enough water for a bath, you would have to raise the temperature of twenty-five gallons of water about fifty degrees. This would require three million calories of heat energy. These three million calories, in the form of free energy, would be enough to lift a weight of one hundred pounds straight up into the air a distance of twelve and a half miles.

How to Make Heat Draw Oxygen Out of the Air

Light a candle and stand it in the center of a soup plate. Fasten it firmly in place with a few drops of melted wax. Then fill the plate almost completely full of water. When the candle is burning steadily, cover it with a milk bottle.

The candle will immediately start to heat the air inside the bottle and make it expand. Trying to escape, some of the air will bubble out into the water in the plate. Then, as though by magic, the water will start to climb right up into the bottle. After it has risen nearly to the top of the candle, the candle will suddenly go out.

What makes the candle go out? The answer is lack of oxygen. As the candle burns, the oxygen in the air inside the bottle is used up. The flame must have oxygen to burn, so after a while it goes out.

Because the oxygen is gone, the remaining air in the bottle has a lower pressure than the outside air. Then the outside air, pushing against the water in the plate, forces it up into the bottle.

How to Show That a Hot Flame Has a Cold Center

This experiment demonstrates a very strange fact about flame. Though most of it is too hot to touch without burning your fingers, there is a cold spot in its center.

The flame of a candle is not made of burning wax, as you might suppose, but is burning gas. In order to burn, a substance must be changed to a gas. This is done by heating it.

Candle wax is made of oily and fatty substances containing carbon and hydrogen. When you light a candle, the wax is drawn up to the burning wick by capillary action. The heat from the wick turns the wax into a gas in the same way heat turns water into steam.

The wax vapor forms the unlighted area of the flame just above the wick. There is no combustion there because there is no oxygen. It is not until the vapor spreads out and joins the oxygen in the air that it begins to burn. This is why a candle flame consists of a hot outer layer of burning wax vapor, with a cool area inside it.

You can prove that this is so by lighting a candle and holding a matchstick in the flame for a moment or two. When you remove the matchstick, you will see that it has been burned at two places—where the two hot outside parts of the flame touched it. The part between these two places will not be burned.

Another way to do this experiment is to hold a small square of stiff paper horizontally and move it quickly through a candle flame about a quarter of an inch above the top of the wick. Hold it steady in the flame for a fraction of a second, but don't let it catch fire. When you remove the paper, there will be a scorched ring on it formed by the hot outside ring of the flame. The center of the ring, which was above the cool part of the flame, will be unscorched.

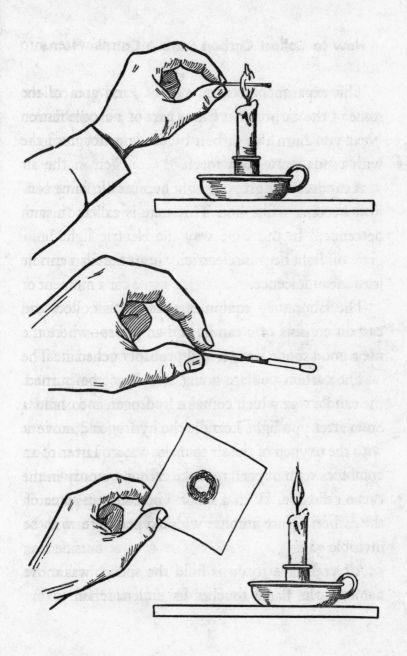

How to Collect Carbon from a Candle Flame

This experiment is in two parts. First you collect some of the carbon that forms part of a candle flame. Next you burn the carbon by feeding oxygen to it with a soda-straw blow torch.

A candle flame gives off light because bits of carbon in it become white hot. This state is called "incandescence." In the same way the electric light bulb gives off light because electricity heats the filaments in it to incandescence.

The laboratory equipment needed to collect the carbon consists of a candle and an old spoon. Don't use a good spoon since it will probably get stained.

The carbon you are going to collect comes from the candle wax which contains hydrogen and carbon. Soon after you light a candle the hydrogen combines with the oxygen of the air to make water. The carbon combines with oxygen to make carbon monoxide and carbon dioxide. With a spoon you can trap some of the carbon before it unites with oxygen to form these invisible gases.

All you have to do is hold the spoon beside the flame so the flame touches its underside for a few seconds. The spoon will then be coated with carbon. This carbon is commonly known as lampblack. If you had allowed the carbon to stay in the flame, it would have been heated until it glowed and formed part of the flame.

With a homemade blowtorch, you can heat the carbon hot enough to burn. Make the blowtorch by flattening one end of a straw and bending the flat part back on itself three times. Fasten the folds with gummed tape. Then make a pinhole in the straw near the folds.

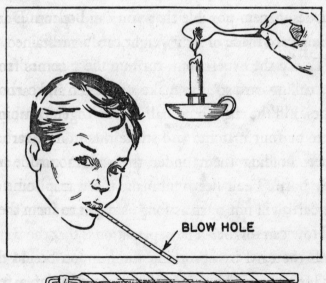

BLOW HOLE

FLATTENED STRAW

Dip the straw in water. Then hold it close to the candle flame and blow through it so that air is forced out through the pinhole against the flame. This will make the flame shoot out to one side. Hold the spoon so this flame strikes the carbon on the spoon's underside. The oxygen you add to the flame will make it so hot that it will soon burn up the carbon. It is the same principle that is used in a regular blowtorch.

How to Boil Water in a Calling Card

Does it seem possible that you can boil water in a calling card made of lightweight cardboard?

To try the experiment, turn up the sides and ends of a calling card so as to make a little tray with raised edges. Fill the tray about half full of water. Then get three or four matches and strike them one after the other, holding them under the calling card while they burn. Their heat will make the water boil, and the card will not burn as long as water remains in it.

How can this be? The explanation is that the water cools the card by absorbing the heat and keeps the card from getting hot enough to burn. More than 212

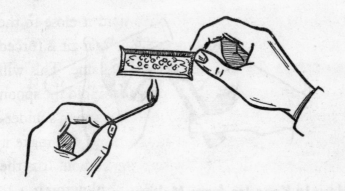

degrees Fahrenheit of heat, which is the boiling point of water, would be needed to set the card on fire. The temperature of the water never gets higher than 212 degrees Fahrenheit because once water reaches its boiling point it stays there. Any further heat applied to it is used to change the water into steam, and the steam carries off the extra heat. In the experiment, the heat goes right through the card and is absorbed by the water.

You can also do this experiment by placing a lighted candle in an empty can, filling a paper plate with water, and putting it on top of the can. To make the experiment work properly, you should punch holes in the sides of the can near the top and bottom. The holes at the bottom will admit fresh air, and those at the top will let the heated gases escape.

How to Keep Ice from Melting in Boiling Water

Put a small lump of ice in the bottom of a test tube or a glass vial (obtainable at a drugstore) and fill the tube or vial with water. Then tilt it and hold a candle under its upper end. In a few minutes the water at the heated end will boil, but the ice at the bottom will remain unmelted. This is possible only because water is such a poor conductor of heat.

How to Cut a String with Heat

Heat waves can easily pass through glass, as anyone knows who has sat indoors next to a closed window on a hot day! Heat also can be concentrated by letting it pass through a magnifying glass. You can

66

use these facts about heat to do an experiment that will amuse your friends.

Tie a short piece of thread around a thumbtack. Push the thumbtack into the bottom of a cork and put the cork in a small bottle. Then tell a friend, "I bet I can cut that piece of string in two without taking it out of the bottle." When your friend finally decides that this is impossible, you show him how it is done.

All you need to do is to focus the rays of the sun onto the string by means of a magnifying glass or "burning glass." You can get a glass of this kind at the ten-cent store. In a few minutes the concentrated heat will burn the string in two.

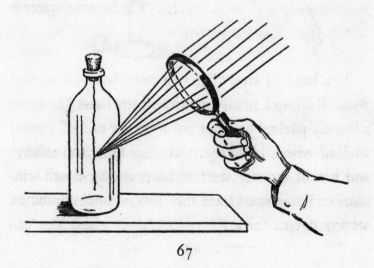

How to Make Steel Burn

Some things—paper, for instance—catch fire very easily. Wood and coal are harder to ignite, though powdered coal burns very quickly. This is because it mixes very quickly and easily in powdered form with the oxygen in the air.

You would find it just about impossible to make a bar of steel burn because it is so hard and solid that it won't combine with oxygen quickly enough. But if you use steel in another form, you can make it burn.

The kind of steel that will burn for you is steel wool. Roll up a small quantity of steel wool to form a loosely packed ball and put it on the end of a small stick of wood. Hold the steel wool in a candle flame and it will quickly start to burn and give off little sparks. These sparks are tiny bits of steel combined with oxygen.

How to Make Heat Expand Metal

The seesaw gadget shown in the drawing provides a striking method of demonstrating that heat expands metals.

The principal part of the device consists of a brass curtain rod or a piece of stiff copper wire stuck through the center of a large flat cork or a matchbox. Do not use a steel wire because steel is a slow conductor of heat. Push two long needles or nails into the sides of the cork or box so that it will pivot on them. At each end of the rod push on a cork and insert pins or tacks in them until the seesaw balances exactly.

Rest the seesaw on the bottoms of two glasses, and light a candle under one end of the rod. The heat will soon make the rod expand, and this will upset the seesaw's balance. The heated end will slowly fall. If you remove the candle, the rod will cool, contract, and balance. By moving the candle from one end of the seesaw to the other, you can keep the seesaw in almost constant motion.

How to Stop Heat from Passing through Holes

Ask a friend some time if he thinks heat will go through a hole. He is sure to say, "Yes." It is the only natural answer. Then tell him that you know some scientific facts about heat and how it acts, and you can use them to stop heat from passing through holes.

To do this experiment you will need a candle and an old strainer or a small piece of wire screen. Light the candle and, when the flame is going well, put the strainer down on top of the flame. Instead of going right through the holes, the flame will be stopped short. Only a little smoke and a fraction of the candle flame's heat will pass through the holes in the strainer.

The explanation is that metal wire is an excellent conductor of heat. It carries away the heat and prevents it from rising up through the strainer.

How to Make Metal Put Out a Candle

Another experiment that will demonstrate how efficiently some metals conduct heat can be performed with a special candle extinguisher.

Copper conducts heat very well, and the extinguisher should be made from a piece of copper wire. Wind the wire about eight times around a broom handle or some other circular object, so that it forms a narrow coil like the one shown in the drawing. Then light a candle and drop the coil over the flame so that it does not touch the flame but completely surrounds it.

In a few minutes the flame will die down and go out. This happens because the copper rapidly absorbs all the heat from the flame, prevents it from vaporizing the wax, and in the end puts it out entirely.

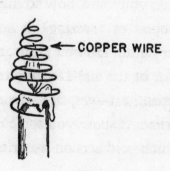

← COPPER WIRE

CONJURING WITH COLD

WE ALL KNOW that cold air freezes water and turns
it into ice. But do you know how strangely water acts
during the process of freezing? It acts differently
from any other liquid. Do you know, too, why cold
forces water out of the air? Do you know how you
can make ice steal heat—yes, *heat*—from nearby ice?

These experiments show you some of the surprising ways in which cold acts on water, air, and ice.

How to Make Cold Drive Water Out of the Air

Take a handful of air—well, no, that wouldn't work. But it is easy enough to take a glassful of air. You don't have to "pour" any air into the glass, of course. It pours itself because of constant downward pressure. And the air contains a good deal of water.

In this experiment you are going to apply cold to the air in the glass and make the cold drive out some of the water.

Fill a glass half full of water and let the water stay in the glass a few minutes until it is room temperature. Then slowly add cracked ice or ice cubes to the water and stir it with a spoon. Very soon the coldness of the water will cool the air surrounding the glass. It will drive the moisture out of this air and some of it will condense in drops on the sides of the glass.

Cold air just can't hold as much moisture as warm air. A cubic foot of air that is at a temperature of eighty degrees Fahrenheit can hold about eleven grains of water vapor. If you lower the temperature to fifty degrees, the same amount of air can hold only four grains of water vapor. The cold drives seven grains of moisture out of the air.

How to Make Ice Steal Heat from Ice

To prepare for this experiment, get a piece of thin wire about ten inches long. Twist each end around a pencil so that the pencils will form handles you can hold in your hands.

Now put an ice cube on top of a bottle. Put the wire across it and push down hard on the two pencils. You will find it easy to push the wire all the way down through the cube. But the cube will still be in one solid piece!

How come? The scientific fact is that the pressure of the wire made the ice directly under the wire melt. In other words, the pressure caused heat. Then, as the ice melted, it stole heat from the colder unmelted ice next to it. This ice became colder still and froze the water almost as soon as it had melted.

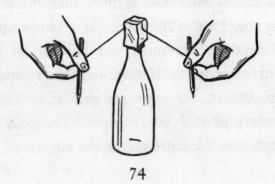

How to Make Cold Break a Bottle

We have seen that heat expands air and other substances and makes them lighter and that cold contracts them and makes them heavier. But when you turn water into ice by applying cold to it, this rule does not apply!

When you first apply cold to water, its temperature drops and it contracts and gets heavier. This continues until water gets as cold as thirty-nine degrees Fahrenheit above zero. Then the rule changes and reverses itself. Below thirty-nine degrees, water starts to expand and get lighter. When it gets as cold as thirty-two degrees Fahrenheit—its freezing point—it is at its coldest and its lightest point. At thirty-two degrees water changes to ice and expands a little bit more. The force exerted by water as it expands is tremendous—quite as powerful as that of metal expanding under intense heat.

You can demonstrate to your friends how powerful the expansive force of water is by an easy but quite dramatic experiment. First get a bucket or a large earthenware jar and fill it with chopped ice and salt, as though you were going to make ice cream. Then take a medium-sized medicine bottle that has a screw cap and fill it with water. Look at the top part of the water. If there are any air bubbles, pour out a little water to get rid of them.

Now screw on the cap tightly and put the bottle in the ice bucket. Put a bath towel over the ice to prevent cold from escaping. In a few minutes the cold will do its work and will turn the water into ice. At that point you will hear a loud pop, showing that the experiment has been a success.

What has happened is that the water, in changing to ice, has expanded and broken the bottle.

How to Make Evaporation Produce Cold

You can demonstrate the scientific principle that evaporation removes heat by using a thermometer and a little rubbing alcohol, a liquid which evaporates quickly. Put some of the alcohol in the palm of your left hand and rest the bulb of the thermometer in it. Then blow across the alcohol to speed up its rate of evaporation. As the alcohol evaporates it will remove heat from the thermometer bulb and quickly bring down the temperature by several degrees.

If you have gone camping, you may have taken along a porous cloth bucket in which to cool water. It does so because of evaporation. The moisture that seeps through the cloth is changed into vapor by the outside air. The vapor carries away some of the heat in the water and thus makes it cool.

The same principle operates when you are perspiring and stand in a cool breeze. Your perspiration is changed into vapor by the cool air. The vapor steals heat from your body and makes you feel chilly.

LIGHT WAVES—THE FASTEST THINGS IN THE WORLD

LIGHT travels in waves, just as heat and sound do. Scientists have measured light waves and have found that they are very short, only a very small fraction of an inch long.

When a searchlight, an electric bulb, a candle, or anything else gives off light, tiny particles, called "photons," radiate from it in all directions. We see these photons as rays of light. Light rays travel at a very fast rate of speed—about 186,000 miles a second.

Even though light rays move at such a tremendous speed, you can experiment with them in a number of interesting ways. You can reflect them, bend them, scatter them, and make them do other things at your bidding in the following experiments.

How Light Can Make It Impossible to See through Water

Can you see through clear, clean water? Of course you can, you think. But here is an experiment which proves that under certain conditions you cannot see through clear water no matter how hard you try. Light waves will make it impossible.

Fill a glass nearly full of water and hold the glass a little above the level of your eyes. Look up through the side of the glass at the underside of the surface of the water. Can you see through to the ceiling? No. The surface of the water seems to have turned into a mirror or a solid piece of shiny metal.

This is due to the fact that when light rays from below strike the underside of the water surface, they can't get through the water at all. They are bent back or reflected into the water.

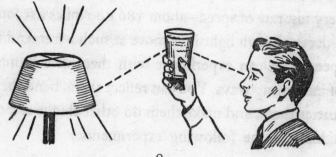

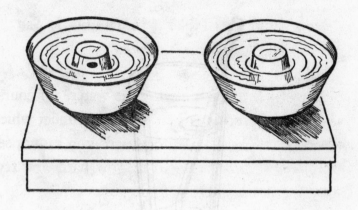

How to Use Light to Make a Coin Vanish

Fill a deep dish with water and drop a penny into it. Cover the penny with a small glass, letting the glass fill with water as you put it in place. The penny will still be in plain sight.

Now lift the glass and replace it, this time lowering it straight down so that the air in it keeps the water out. Then look at the glass from one side and the penny will be invisible. This is because the water bends back the light rays coming toward you from the penny at the point where they leave the air in the glass and strike the water in the dish.

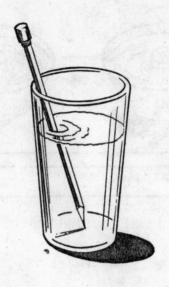

How Water Bends Light Waves

Light usually travels in straight lines unless it is bent by an external object in its way. This bending is called refraction. When light waves enter water, they are slowed up because the water is denser than air. Glass also slows up light. Scientists have calculated that because light passes more slowly through glass than through air, a person wearing glasses sees things two trillionths of a second later than one who doesn't!

When a ray of light enters water at an angle, the slowing up also makes them change their direction. You can demonstrate this by putting a pencil on a slant into a glass that is about two-thirds full of water. Hold the glass so that your eyes are on a level with the surface of the water. The pencil will then seem to be broken where it enters the water. This is because the light reflected from the pencil becomes bent as it passes from the air into the water.

Bent Light Rays Cause an Odd Illusion

This is another experiment that shows in a very interesting way how water slows up and bends light rays.

All you need for the experiment is a glass that is filled nearly to the brim with water. Put the glass on a table and look straight down into it. If you have never done this before, you will probably be surprised, for the bottom of the glass and the part of the table you see through it will look as though they are raised an inch or more above the rest of the table.

This effect is caused by the fact that the light waves

coming up from the bottom of the glass are bent at the surface of the water. This makes them seem to start their journey from a point that is about an inch above the actual bottom of the glass.

How to Bend Light in a Curve

With a simple piece of homemade equipment, you can make light rays obey your wishes and bend in the form of a curve. You do this by making them follow a stream of water which holds the rays almost as though it were a solid metal tube.

The apparatus for the experiment is made from a glass jar with a metal screw cap, a piece of dark cloth or dark paper (heavy brown wrapping paper will do), and a flashlight.

Punch two holes in the cap of the jar, one in the center and the other near the edge. Fill the jar with water, screw on the cap, and then wrap the cloth or paper around the jar so that it extends below the bottom, as shown in the drawing.

Hold the jar over a sink and push the lighted flashlight under the dark cover against the bottom of the

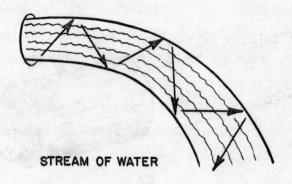

STREAM OF WATER

jar. Then darken the room you are in. Tilt the jar so the water flows out of the center hole in its cover and put your finger in the stream close to the hole. Light from the flashlight will strike your finger. Move your finger farther down the curved stream of water, and the light will continue to strike it. The water is bending the light in a curve.

The diagram shows how the water bends the light. The surface of the stream of water acts as a reflector, just as if it were a mirror or a piece of shiny metal. The light waves bounce back and forth inside the stream, from side to side. Some of the light escapes, but most of it stays inside the water.

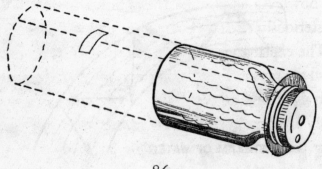

Using Light to Make the Invisible Visible

Put a penny in a bowl and put the bowl on a bookcase or shelf that is nearly at the level of your eyes. Then walk backwards away from the bowl until the penny is just hidden from sight by the bowl's rim. Stop there and ask a friend to pour water into the bowl. As he does so, the penny will slowly and mysteriously rise and come into full view!

The explanation is that when there is water in the bowl the rays of light from the penny do not travel in a straight line between the penny and your eyes. They are bent at the surface of the water just where they pass from the water to the air.

The Strange Silver Egg Experiment

This is an amusing experiment to show to your friends.

First blacken an egg all over by holding it near a candle flame until it is coated with carbon. Then put it in a bowl of water. It will look as if it were covered with silver. Show the egg to a friend and ask him to take it out of the water. To his surprise, the beautiful silver egg will instantly turn into a sooty black one!

The explanation of why the egg looks silver is simple. The carbon, consisting of very finely divided particles, is not wetted by the water and holds a very fine film of air. This acts as a mirror and reflects a silvery light.

How to Show Why the Sky Looks Blue

Did you ever stop to wonder why the sky has a beautiful blue color?

The sun's light is white, which means that it contains all the colors of the spectrum—red, orange, yellow, green, blue, and violet. The light waves given off by the blue and violet rays are short and are more easily bent away from a straight line than the longer waves. Dust and moisture in the air bend the blue and violet rays and scatter them. This makes it possible for us to see them more clearly than the other colors, and it is this that makes the sky look blue to us.

You can show how this bending and scattering takes place by the following experiment. Fill a glass with water and put a few drops of milk in it. The milk represents the dust and moisture in the air.

Now darken the room and hold an electric flashlight close to the glass. Look at the glass from one side, at a right angle to the beam of the flashlight. The liquid will appear to be blue because the particles of milk have scattered the short blue rays in the light of the flashlight.

How to Make Light Change Red to Green

This experiment illustrates a strange characteristic of light that is called "selective reflection." This means that, at different angles, light will reflect to your eyes different parts of the same substance. At one angle it will select and reflect one substance, and at another angle, another substance.

You can demonstrate this by using red ink or mercurochrome. Hold a drinking glass upside down, and pour a small amount of red ink onto its bottom. Look straight down at the ink and it will be red. Then shift the glass to make the light waves from the ink reflect into your eye at an angle, as is shown in the drawing. The red ink or mercurochrome will instantly change to green!

TAMING THE SOUND WAVES

How DOES the sound of a clock striking or of a dog barking get to your ears? You can make a simple— though not quite exact—illustration of how sound travels by dropping a stone into a pond or dropping a cake of soap into the water in a bathtub. Little waves will spread out in all directions. Sound travels through the air in much the same way, spreading out in all directions in the form of waves.

Sound waves are produced by an object that is vibrating, or moving rapidly to and fro. Our ears can hear sound waves that vibrate from about fifteen times a second to 20,000 times a second.

A vibrating object transmits its vibrations, as sound waves, to the air particles that surround it. These pass on the waves through millions of other particles until the original energy is exhausted.

Sound travels through dry air at a speed of 1,087 feet a second. Generally speaking, they travel better in liquids and solids than in air. They go nearly four times as fast through water—4,708 feet a second. This is why distant sounds seem nearer and clearer on a damp day and why sound travels clearly for long distances over a lake or other water. Sound speeds up a great deal when it goes through solids, traveling at a rate of 16,400 feet a second through steel and 18,000 feet a second through glass.

You can learn many interesting facts about sound waves by doing the experiments in this section.

How to Hear the "Sound of the Sea" in a City

Almost everyone at some time or other has held a sea shell to his ear and has heard the muffled, rumbling sound that is like the sound of waves breaking against the shore.

If you know your science, you will know that this is not really the sound of the sea. It is the sound of the air inside the shell vibrating in response to sound waves in the air outside. You will hear particularly loud "sea sounds" in a noisy city or town.

You do not need a shell to hear these sounds. Drinking glasses, tin cans, vases, and other similar objects are just as good or even better. The sounds will be deep when you use a fairly large object and will be high and shrill when you use a small one.

Sending Sounds by Radio

You can send sound waves through the air like radio waves. Your broadcasting station is a milk bottle, and the receiving station is another bottle of the same size and shape.

Tell a friend to hold a milk bottle close to his right ear, but not flat up against it. Sit at his right side, just beside him, and blow across the mouth of your bottle. This will make the air inside your bottle vibrate and make a low whistling sound. Your friend will hear the same sound, only not quite so loud, coming from the inside of his bottle.

The sound in your friend's bottle is produced in the same way as a "sound of the sea" is produced in a shell or a drinking glass.

How to Magnify the Sound of Heartbeats

It will take you only a minute or two to make a homemade stethoscope through which you can clearly hear heartbeats. A stethoscope of this kind demonstrates the scientific fact that sounds are magnified when they pass through a tube. This is due partly to the fact that the sound waves are concentrated within a small space.

The stethoscope is made by fitting a kitchen funnel into one end of a piece of rubber tubing about three feet long. The tubing from an old bathroom shower spray is excellent for this purpose. Put the funnel over your heart and the other end of the tubing in your ear, and you will hear your heartbeats very distinctly. Then listen to a friend's heartbeats or put the funnel over a watch placed on a table and see how much the stethoscope magnifies its ticking.

You can demonstrate this same principle by using a piece of paper rolled up to form a tube. Put a watch on the table and listen to its ticking through the tube. You will be surprised at how much louder it sounds.

How to Make Sound Put Out a Candle

Scientists have been experimenting for some time with what they call "sound rings." These are whirling rings produced by sound vibrations which have great power. Sound rings have been produced that can knock a person down at a distance of twenty feet!

No practical use has yet been found for these rings, but they might be used to carry smoke from factory chimneys into the upper atmosphere in order to free cities of soot.

It is very easy to make sound rings at home and to demonstrate how strong they are by using them to blow out a candle. Get a circular cardboard box, such as an oatmeal box. Cut a round hole exactly the size of a penny in the center of the cover. Fasten the cover tightly on the box with gummed tape.

Set the box on a table and put a lighted candle three feet in front of it. Point the hole in the box top at the flame and then tap the bottom of the box sharply. This will make invisible sound rings issue from the hole and put out the candle. Move the candle farther away and repeat the experiment. It is possible to put out the flame at a distance as great as six feet.

If you want to see the rings in action, light a damp paper towel. When it is smoldering, put it in the box for a moment or two to fill the box with smoke. The smoke will make the rings visible, and you will be able to see them whirling rapidly around.

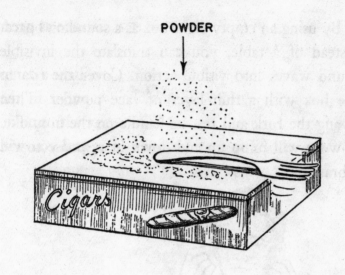

POWDER

How to Use Sound Waves to Make Powder Dance

You can make a fork vibrate and give off a singing note by plucking one of its prongs with your finger and then resting the handle on a table. The table top will act as a sounding board and will increase the musical sound made by the fork. The vibrations from the fork are transmitted to the wood, and the sound waves which it produces hit the drum of your ear and make it vibrate so you hear the sounds.

By using an empty cigar box as a sounding board, instead of a table, you can translate the invisible sound waves into visible action. Cover the top of the box with a thin layer of face powder. Then twang the fork and rest its handle on the box. The powder will jump up and down in response to the vibrations.

How to Use String to Speed Up Sound Waves

This experiment enables you to make sound waves louder—to your own ears at least—by making them travel along a piece of string.

Get a piece of string about five feet long, and a silver tablespoon. Tie the spoon to the middle of the string, and then push each end of the string in one of your ears. Now swing the spoon so that it strikes against a table or some other piece of furniture. You will hear a surprisingly loud sound, like the tone of a big bell. If you use three spoons or a spoon and two forks, you will get a medley of different booming bell-like sounds.

Pencil-and-String Artillery

Another good experiment to show how easily sound travels along a string is done with a pencil and a piece of string about six feet long. Make a loop two feet long at one end of the string, and at the other end make a loop just large enough to hold a pencil tightly.

Ask a friend to cover his ears with the palms of his hands and put the large loop over his head and hands. Put a pencil in the small loop and draw the string tight. Holding the pencil at top and bottom, turn it slowly around. The sound of the pencil's movements will be magnified so much that it will sound like gunfire to the listener.

You can produce other surprising noises, such as thunder and breaking waves, by rubbing the back of a knife or a piece of folded paper along the string or by flicking the string with your finger.

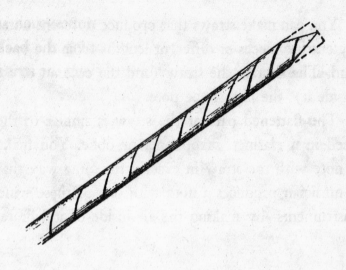

How to Make a Straw Clarinet

With an ordinary soda straw you can demonstrate very clearly how vibrations produce sound waves. Take a straw and flatten one end for a distance of half an inch. Then cut a small slanting piece from both corners as shown in the drawing. Put the other end of the straw in your mouth and blow into it hard. Your breath will make the flattened part move rapidly to and fro, and this will make the air inside the straw vibrate and produce a musical note, something like that of a tin horn.

You can make straws that produce different notes by cutting pieces of different lengths from the open end. The shorter the straw (and the column of air inside it), the higher the note.

The flattened part of the straw is similar to the reed in a clarinet, saxophone, or oboe. You make a note with the straw in exactly the same way that a musician produces a note with one of these wind instruments—by making the air inside of it vibrate.

PLAYING WITH GRAVITY

EVERYBODY knows that gravity is the force that pulls things down to the earth, making apples and leaves fall down from trees.

Everything from a piece of paper to your own body has a center of gravity. This is the point at which the object will balance.

As long as the center of gravity is supported, the object cannot fall over. That is why the famous Leaning Tower of Pisa doesn't tumble over. A straight line drawn from its center of gravity to the ground will go through a point within its base. For this reason, the base supports the center of gravity. If the tower leaned so far to one side that its center of gravity was not above its base, it would fall over.

Gravity is fascinating—and there are some interesting experiments that demonstrate little-known facts about it.

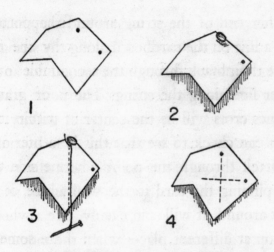

How to Find the Center of Gravity

It is easy to find the center of gravity of an object like a baseball bat, a book, or a banana. All you have to do is to rest it on your finger and move it until it balances. But how would you find the center of gravity of an irregularly shaped piece of cardboard like the one shown in the drawing? Here is how to do it.

Cut a piece of cardboard into any odd shape, and make two pencil dots on it at different places near its edge. Put a thumbtack through one of the dots and pin the card to the wall. Fasten a nail or some other small object to one end of a string, then wind the other end of the string around the thumbtack. Draw a line on the cardboard along the string. Next put the thumbtack through the second dot and draw another line along the string. The point where the two lines cross will be the center of gravity.

You can check to see that this is so by putting a thumbtack through the point where the two lines cross, pinning the card to the wall again, and spinning it around. It will spin evenly, like a wheel, and will stop at different places when the momentum is used up. But put the thumbtack at any other point and the cardboard will be out of balance. It will spin unevenly and will always stop at the same place —where its center of gravity is in the lowest possible position.

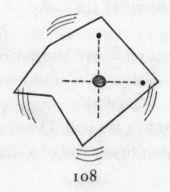

A Gravity-Defying Experiment

If you want to keep something in balance—for example, a pencil—you must find its center of gravity and balance it at that point. Then it will stay put without tipping or toppling over.

The center of gravity of a pencil or a straight stick is at its middle. You can prove this by tying a piece of string to the middle of a pencil. If you hold the string, the pencil will stay in a straight line without tipping to one side or the other. You could do the same thing by resting the middle of a pencil on top of a small stick or even on the head of a pin. The rule is that as long as the support (the string or the stick) is at the center of gravity, the object will stay level.

This experiment is one that appears to defy this rule—to defy the law of gravity.

Push a nail into the bottom of a cork, and then push the prongs of two forks into the cork. Now balance the nail on the rim of a glass, as in the drawing. It looks as though the weight of the forks should throw the whole thing out of balance and pull the cork down. The nail looks as if it is off balance. In fact, the whole thing looks impossible!

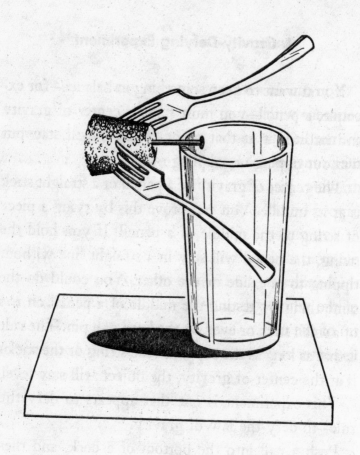

Actually, the center of gravity of the whole apparatus is just beneath the rim of the glass where the nail is resting. That is why it stays in balance.

Another Balancing Experiment

You can do another surprising gravity-defying experiment with a cork, a needle, and two forks. Push the needle into the bottom of the cork and then push the prongs of the forks into the cork, as shown in the drawing. Place the point of the needle on top of a capped bottle, and it will balance perfectly.

You might think that the heavy forks would topple over the whole arrangement. Actually, however, the handles of the forks lower the center of gravity of the whole group of objects to a point below the tip of the needle. The arrangement balances because its center of gravity is in line with its point of support.

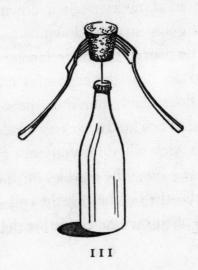

How Gravity Conquers Speed

Which will reach the earth first—a bullet shot from a gun or a bullet dropped to the ground from the same height as the gun? Most people are apt to think that the second bullet will reach the ground first, for the bullet from the gun has a long way to go before it finishes its flight and comes to rest.

Though it is hard to believe, both bullets will hit the earth at exactly the same moment. All objects, if the air resistance is the same, fall toward the earth at the same rate of speed. This law of gravity is not altered by the fact that an object—such as the bullet shot from the gun—may be traveling horizontally through the air. Gravity pulls it down just as fast as if it were going straight down.

This can be proved by the following experiment. Put two marbles near the edge of a table standing on the bare floor. Each should be the same distance from the edge. Then hold a hacksaw blade near them, as shown. (A stick will do if you can't get hold of a hacksaw blade.) Snap the marbles off the table.

One marble—the one nearest the end of the blade or stick—will be thrown much farther than the other.

But both marbles will hit the floor at the same instant. You can hear the sound of the marbles as they strike the floor.

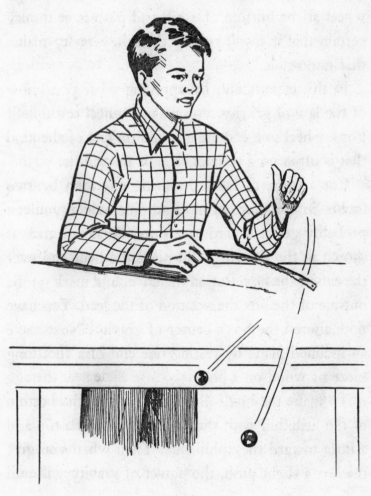

How to Make a Wheel Roll Uphill

If you stand a wheel at the top of a hill and give it a push, it will roll downhill. But if you stand a wheel at the bottom of a hill and push it, it is very certain that it *won't* roll up the hill. Gravity makes that impossible.

In this experiment, by applying what you know of the law of gravity, you make a wheel roll uphill! For a wheel you can use a round tin box of the kind that is often used to contain nuts or candies.

Cut a piece of lead measuring one inch by two inches from a piece of old lead pipe, which you can probably get at a hardware store. Bend one end, as shown in the drawing, and place the bent end over the rim of the box. Put on the cover and mark on the outside of the box the position of the lead. You have now altered the box's center of gravity. Next make an inclined plane by resting one end of a foot-long piece of wood on a book.

To make the box roll uphill, put it at the bottom of the little hill with the lead weight at the top and a little toward the uphill side. Then when you give the box a slight push, the power of gravity will pull

COVER

on the lead and make the box roll up the hill. This experiment illustrates an important rule of mechanics —that all objects tend to move so that their center of gravity is in the lowest possible position.

Checking Galileo's Theories

Which falls faster, a cannonball or a lemon? For centuries everybody believed that a heavy object would fall much faster than a light one. But Galileo, the Italian astronomer and physicist who was born almost four hundred years ago, proved that light and heavy objects fall at the same speed by dropping balls of different weights from the Leaning Tower of Pisa.

You can prove this for yourself right away by dropping two objects such as a book and a pencil from the same height. They will both reach the floor at the same instant. This rule holds absolutely true only when the objects are dropped in a vacuum. But it is almost as true when the objects are dropped in air, provided there is not too great a difference in weight between the two objects and the distance they are dropped is not too far.

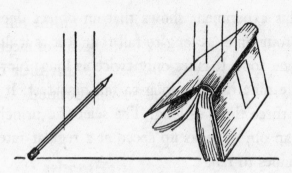

Here is another experiment that shows the way falling objects pick up speed when they are dropped. To do it you will need a piece of string ten feet long and four potatoes or apples.

Tie one potato to one end of the string. Tie the next one at a distance of one foot from this end, the next one three feet farther along, and the last one five feet beyond that. Then stand on a chair and hold the free end of the string so the bottom potato is just clear of the floor.

Now let go of the string and listen for the bumps as the potatoes hit the floor. The length of time between each bump will be exactly the same, in spite of the fact that the potatoes are not evenly spaced along the string. Actually, the bottom potato falls a couple of inches, the next one falls one foot, the next one four feet, and the last one nine feet.

This experiment shows that an object does not take four times as long to fall four feet as it does to fall one foot. It takes only twice as long. Nor does it take nine times as long to fall nine feet. It takes only three times as long. The scientific principle is that an object picks up speed at a regular rate as it continues to fall.

EXPERIMENTS WITH ELECTRICITY

ELECTRICITY was first talked about 2,500 years ago when the Greek philosopher Thales rubbed a piece of amber with woolen cloth and found that small particles of wool stuck to the amber. The unknown and invisible force that made this happen has been named "electricity," from the Greek word for amber.

You or any other experimental scientist can generate electricity in the same way that Thales did—

even though you may not have a piece of amber. Shuffle your feet on a woolen rug and then touch a metal lampstand or radiator. An electric spark will jump from your finger to the metal. The electricity was generated when you rubbed your feet on the rug. This kind of electricity is called "static electricity," and is produced by friction.

Scientists do not know exactly what static electricity is, but they have worked out a theory that seems to explain it.

All substances are believed to be made up of positive electrical particles called "protons" and negative electrical particles called "electrons." When an object is undisturbed, the protons and electrons balance each other. The object then has no electrical charge. But when you rub some objects, they pick up electrons from the material with which they are rubbed. They become negatively charged. Other objects give off electrons to the material rubbed against them. These are positively charged.

Static electricity is fun to experiment with, but it is not very useful. It was only when men learned how to make electricity by means of batteries and to lead the electricity along wires that electricity became important. By moving electricity along wires it can be made to turn motors, light lamp bulbs, operate telephones and radio sets, and do many other useful things.

The principle behind making a battery that produces electricity was discovered by accident by an Italian physician named Luigi Galvani, who lived at the end of the eighteenth century. One day, when he was dissecting the leg of a frog, he found that the dead frog's muscle twitched when it touched two pieces of metal: copper and iron. His friend and fellow scientist, Count Alessandro Volta, realized that the movement was caused by electric charges produced by the metals. With this in mind, Volta made the first electric battery. It was a pile of zinc and copper disks separated by pieces of leather soaked in salt water. Volta had discovered that an electric current is produced when two different metals are separated by something moist.

Every electric battery consists of two plates, or pieces of material that will carry a current, placed in a solution that will also carry a current. You can make a battery, for example, by putting a strip of copper and a strip of zinc in a glass of salt water. It will have a strength of about one and a half volts (units of electric force), or roughly the same amount of power a flashlight battery has. Its strength depends on the materials used and the kind of solution in which they are placed.

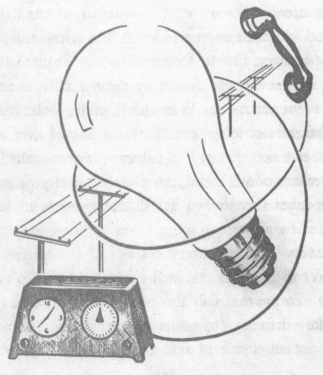

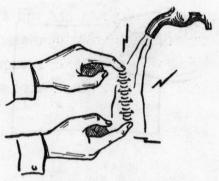

How to Make a Volta Battery

You can make a battery like the one Volta originated without any trouble at all. Instead of zinc and copper disks, you use five pennies and five dimes.

First get a piece of blotting paper and let it soak for a few minutes in a saucepan containing salt water. Make the salt water by adding half a cupful of salt to a pan half full of plain water. Cut the blotting paper into one-inch squares. Then pile up the pennies and dimes alternately—first a penny, then a dime—and put a piece of blotting paper between each pair of coins.

When the pile is completed, you have a Volta battery. To prove that it produces electricity, hold the battery between your fingers under water. You will get a small electric shock!

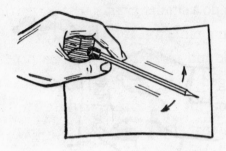

Generating Electricity in Paper and Balloons

Take a sheet of stiff paper and hold it against a smooth wall of your home with your left hand. Then rub it briskly with your right hand for a few seconds. The friction of the rubbing will generate a charge of electricity in the paper and it will stick to the wall, held there by the attraction between the electricity and the neutral wall.

Now pull the paper away from the wall and you will hear a crackling sound. This is really a miniature reproduction of the thunder of an electrical storm. Flashes of lightning are nothing but huge sparks of static electricity.

You can do a similar experiment by putting a piece of paper on a table top and rubbing the flat side of a pencil back and forth across it. The paper will become charged with electricity and will stick to the table. If you lift one corner slightly and then let it go, it will snap back into place, attracted by the neutral table top.

You can also electrify a balloon by rubbing it with a piece of woolen cloth. Do this, then put the balloon against a wall or against your cheek. The balloon will stay in place as if stuck with glue.

Electrified Balloons Don't Like Each Other

With two balloons and a piece of cloth you can conjure up a powerful invisible force and set it to work.

Blow up two balloons and tie each one with a piece of string about eighteen inches long. Then rub each balloon briskly on a piece of woolen cloth. Hold the balloons by their strings, one string in each hand, and try to make them touch each other. They won't do it. Instead, they will do everything they can to avoid touching each other!

It is fun, too, to do this experiment with three balloons. Their antics in avoiding each other are very amusing to watch.

This experiment demonstrates the fact that objects charged with static electricity are repelled by each other.

Electrified Objects Attract Neutral Ones

When you charge an object with static electricity, it attracts neutral objects. Here are two experiments that demonstrate this fact.

Take a pocket comb and charge it with electricity by running it briskly through your hair or by rubbing it on your coat sleeve. Tear a piece of tissue paper into small squares and bring the comb near to them. The papers will jump at the comb and cling to it. They will stay on the comb until its electrical charge grows weak, and then will suddenly jump off.

For the second experiment you need a ping-pong ball. Put it on a table and then charge your comb with

electricity as before. Bring the comb close to the ball.
The neutral ball will be attracted by the comb and
will roll toward it. Keep moving the comb, and the
ball will follow it around the top of the table.

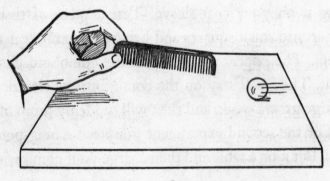

Puffed-Rice Electric Fireworks

Rub a comb with a woolen or silk cloth and then plunge it into a bowl of puffed rice. Draw the comb out and hold it still. A lot of pieces of rice will cling to it, but after a second or two they will absorb electrons from the comb. Then they can't get away fast enough and will pop off in all directions.

If the fireworks aren't as active as they should be, heat the puffed rice in a pan in the oven before doing the experiment.

How to Make Electricity Move Water

This is a very surprising experiment. It shows in an unexpected way the power that electricity can exert.

Stand at a sink and run the cold water. Turn the faucet so that the smallest possible continuous stream of water flows from it. Then charge your comb with electricity by rubbing it on your coat sleeve, and move it slowly toward the water. The electricity in the comb will attract the neutral water. When the comb is about an inch away from the stream, the water will bend over toward the comb. Once you have the water under control, you can make it wriggle like a snake by moving the comb toward it and away from it.

How to "Taste" Electricity

Electricity is invisible and, as a matter of actual fact, it doesn't have a taste. But when electricity flows through salt water or some other liquid conductor it produces chemicals that do have a taste.

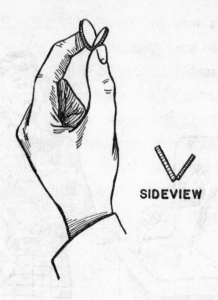

SIDEVIEW

When you taste these, you are "tasting" electricity.

Get a copper penny and a nickel, and give them a thorough cleaning with scouring powder. These are the two metallic plates of a miniature electric cell. Wash them off, and hold the coins so they form a V, with their bottom edges touching. Then put the tip of your tongue inside the V, touching both coins, and you will taste something sharp and bitter. This taste results from the chemical change in your saliva which is produced by the tiny electric current set up by the contact between the saliva on your tongue and the two metals.

Another way to "taste" electricity is to push a straightened steel paper clip and a piece of thin copper wire into a lemon, as shown in the drawing. Hold the ends of the wires close together, but not touching, and put them on your tongue. You will feel a slight tingle and taste something metallic. These are caused by the current of electricity generated by the battery of two different conducting materials and the acid in the lemon.

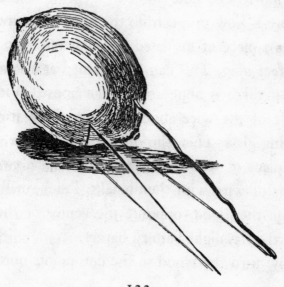

How to Show That Electricity Produces Magnetism

With a flashlight battery and a cheap compass, you can demonstrate the scientific fact that a current of electricity produces magnetism. This fact was discovered about a hundred years ago by a Danish schoolteacher named Hans Oersted. A compass, which points north because it is drawn by magnetic deposits of iron near the North Pole, was on his desk one day when he was doing some experiments. To his surprise, he noticed that when electricity was passed through a wire it forced the needle of the compass to swing to one side.

Here is how you can do the same experiment.

Get a piece of insulated or lacquered wire about four feet long. This can be obtained at a hardware store if there is none around the house. Wind the middle of the wire about a dozen times around a drinking glass. Then slip off the coil of wire, rest it on a piece of wood, and fasten down the two free strands of wire with thumbtacks. Put a small compass on the wood, opposite the center of the coil. Keep the flashlight battery handy.

Now turn the wood so the coil points north and

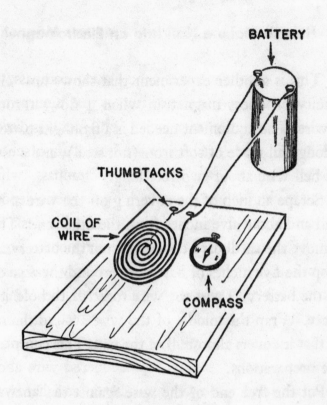

BATTERY

THUMBTACKS

COIL OF
WIRE

COMPASS

south. With a knife, scrape the covering off the free ends of the two wires. Then connect the ends of the two wires to the terminals of the battery, as in the diagram. Electricity will start to flow through the wires and the magnetic force of the current will swing the compass needle to one side.

135

How to Make a Nail into an Electromagnet

This is another experiment that shows how electricity produces magnetism when it flows through a wire. The equipment needed is a flashlight battery, a long nail made of soft iron (not steel), and a piece of bell wire about two feet long.

Scrape an inch of the covering off the wire at one end and about five inches from the other end. Then remove the cardboard covering from the battery and loop the five inches of bare wire around the zinc can of the battery. Twist the wire together to hold it in place. Wrap the middle of the wire around the nail so that it covers almost all of the nail. This completes the preparations.

Put the free end of the wire against the knob on top of the battery. This will start electric current flowing through the wire, and the current will immediately turn the nail into a small electromagnet. Put some pins and paper clips near each end of the nail and the nail will pick them up like a magnet.

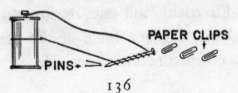

SEEING ISN'T ALWAYS BELIEVING

THE HUMAN EYE has certain limitations, but on the whole it is an amazing mechanism. It adapts itself instantly to all kinds of conditions, brings objects at great or small distances into focus, and is capable of fast and almost unlimited service. In fact, experiments with electric sparks have shown that the eye can see printed letters on a page in forty billionths of a second!

Our eyes are so sensitive that they can respond to the light of a candle fourteen miles away. They contain more than a million delicate elements that are connected to the brain by cablelike bundles of nerves, which carry images from the eyes to the brain.

Your eyes are really miniature cameras that give you a motion picture of what goes on around you. Each eye has a lens inside it that focuses the light on a sensitive back surface, the retina. Nerves leading from the retina carry the message of what you see to the brain. The retina corresponds to the ground-glass screen in an empty camera and to the film in a loaded camera.

The eye, like the camera, has a way to control the amount of light that enters the lens. The pupil, the little round, dark dot in the center of the eye, does this automatically. In bright light the pupil closes down to pin-point size, letting in less light and protecting your eye from the brightness. In semidarkness the pupil opens wide, letting in more light so that you can see more clearly.

Scientists have discovered some strange things about our eyes that are not generally known. These are demonstrated in the following experiments.

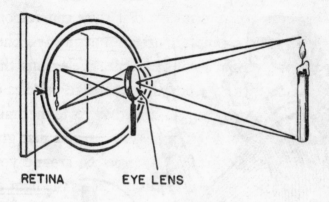

RETINA   EYE LENS

How to Prove That Our Eyes See Images
Upside Down

One of the little-known facts about our eyes is
that they first receive images upside down, just as
does the ground glass in a camera on which the lens
throws an upside-down image of the scene in front
of the lens. By a mysterious process that takes place
in our brains, the upside-down images on the retinas
of our eyes are turned right side up. This experiment
will enable you to reverse this process and see something—a pin—as the eye first sees it.

Make a pinhole in a piece of stiff paper. Hold the
paper about six inches from one eye and look through

the pinhole at an unshaded electric light a few feet away. The room does not have to be darkened. Then hold a pin upright and close to your eye, between the eye and the pinhole. You will see an amazing thing. The pin will appear to be upside down.

What happens is this: The pinhole acts as a lens (like the lens of an eye or a camera) and turns the image of the pin upside down. This makes it appear upright on the retina of your eye instead of the way it normally appears, which is upside down. Your brain then reverses the image as usual on the retina.

How to See a Billionth of an Ounce

If you weigh an ounce of sugar or salt, you can see that it is a very small amount. You can surprise your friends with some hocus-pocus by telling them that you can show them something that weighs only a *billionth* of an ounce.

Roll up a piece of paper to form a tube and fasten it with a rubber band. Then tell a friend that the tube is a special kind of microscope. Tell him to hold it to his right eye and look through it at the page of a book.

When he does this, tell him: "Find a period at the end of a sentence, and look at it. One half of it weighs a billionth of an ounce!"

The weight of a period was discovered by some inquisitive physicists who weighed a piece of paper before and after a single period had been printed on it. Using a very delicate balance, they found that a printed period weighed just about two billionths of an ounce.

The Ghostly Room Experiment

One of the interesting things that scientists have discovered about our eyes is that when the retinas are overstimulated by light they show us what are called "afterimages." For example, if you look at a very bright light such as a bare electric bulb or glaring sunlight, you will notice that an image of the light persists for some time after you look away. It is this same persistence of vision that makes a rapid series of separate pictures blend into smooth action when you watch the movies or television.

You can create an afterimage of a ghostly room very easily. Sit with some friends in a room at night with the window shades pulled down so that no light from outside can enter. Arrange your chairs in a circle around a table or floor lamp, with one person right beside the lamp to turn it on and off.

To make the experiment work well, you must sit in the darkened room for a full ten minutes so that everyone's eyes become used to the darkness. Each person must then look steadily in the general direction of the lamp but not directly at it. Tell your friends to be sure to keep their eyes from moving

during the time the room will be illuminated and immediately afterward.

Now light the lamp and keep it on for one whole second. Turn it off. In a moment you and your friends will see the room in full light again! This impression or afterimage may last for some time. Everything will look exactly as it did when the light was on, and in addition many details will be evident that you did not notice during the brief second the light was on. The effect is really astonishing. Try it and you will see.

How Your Eyes Make the Movies Move

The movies don't really move. It is only our persistence of vision that makes them *seem* to be full of action. When you watch a movie that lasts for an hour, you see a succession of about 57,000 still pictures—sixteen every second. They follow each other so rapidly that they appear to be moving.

Each picture sends a still image to the eye and brain. But while the brain is registering one picture, another one comes along and blends into it. Our

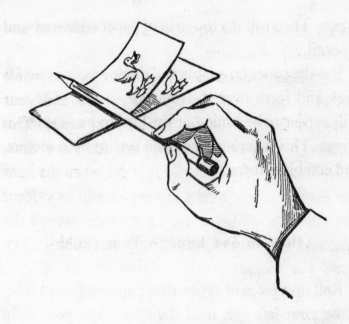

visual impressions do not vanish at once. They fade away gradually.

You can make a simple device that will show how the brain retains the image of a picture and blends two pictures together to give the illusion of motion. Cut a strip of paper about ten inches long and three inches wide and fold it in half lengthwise. Draw a picture of a man or of a bird with folded wings on the bottom strip. Directly over it, on the top strip, draw the man running or the bird with upraised wings. Then roll the top strip of paper tightly around a pencil.

Put the paper on a table and move a pencil quickly back and forth over it, from side to side. The man will appear to be runing or the bird to be flapping its wings. This is because the brain retains both pictures and combines them.

How to See through Your Hand

Roll up a piece of typewriter paper to form a tube. Close your left eye, hold the tube up to your right eye, and look through it. Now put your left hand, with its palm toward you, against the left side of the tube and open your left eye. There will seem to be a large hole in your left hand through which you can see what is behind it!

It is an optical illusion. The right eye is seeing a scene through the tube, while the left eye can't see it because its view is blocked by your left hand. The normal movement of the eyes to focus together on a distant spot moves the right eye's view over to the left.

Each of our eyes sees separately although they work at their best only when both of them are used. With one eye you can't judge distance accurately, but with both eyes you can because the brain is accustomed to judging where the two lines of vision cross. And it is because we have two eyes that we see things in three dimensions.

How to Make Sight Change One Color into Another

This is an interesting experiment that demonstrates a little-known fact about afterimages. This fact is that when you look at a color, the afterimage will be of the complementary color. Red will give a green afterimage, green will give red, orange will give blue, and so on.

You can prove this very easily by putting a small piece of colored paper on a pad of white paper and looking at it steadily for a full minute. At the end of that time, cover the colored paper with a piece of white paper. If you have been looking at red, you will now see a green afterimage of the same size and shape as the red piece of paper.

How to Prove That Our Eyes Have Blind Spots

If you should tell a friend that there is a part of each of his eyes that is blind, he would probably not believe you. Just the same, this is a scientific fact, and you can easily prove it.

Take a piece of white paper and draw on it a

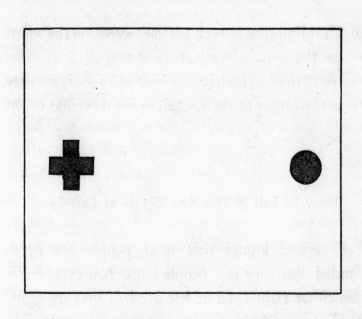

cross and a circle or use the cross and circle illustrated here. They should be about two inches apart. Give the paper to your friend and tell him to hold it about a foot in front of his eyes. Then tell him to close his left eye, look at the cross with his right eye, and move the paper slowly toward him. After he moves the paper a few inches, the circle will suddenly disappear. This is the point at which the light rays coming from it fall on the blind spot of his right eye.

The blind spot in each person's eye is on the retina where the optic nerve leaves the eyeball. It is about one twelfth of an inch in diameter and a short distance from the center of the eyeball in the direction of the nose.

How to Tell if You Are Right- or Left-Eyed

Everyone knows that most people are right-handed. But very few people know that everyone is also either right-eyed or left-eyed. If you are right-eyed, your right eye is the dominant one. It leads in seeing things, and your left eye follows it. It is also the better eye to use in looking through a telescope or aiming a rifle.

Try this experiment to tell if you are right-eyed or left-eyed. Stand and point with your right forefinger at some object (any object) about twelve feet away. Keep both eyes open. Then shut your right eye and watch what happens.

If you are right-eyed, your forefinger will seem to jump quickly to the right. If you are left-eyed, on the other hand, your finger won't move.

WHAT MAKES THE WEATHER?

WE ARE so used to different kinds of weather—fair, windy, cloudy, rainy, and sunny days—that we seldom stop to ask what causes them. Science tells us that all the changes in the weather are caused by changes in the temperature of the air. The heat of the sun, the cooling effects of the oceans, and the cold of the upper air are three of the major forces that make air hot or cold and bring about weather differences.

In these experiments you can imitate Nature's forces and use heat and cold to cause winds, rain, snow, and other phenomena of the weather.

153

How to Show Why the Wind Blows

With an empty shoe box as a laboratory, you can set up a very convincing experiment that shows why the wind blows. The scientific facts of the experiment are as follows:

Wind is caused by differences between the temperatures of masses of air. Cold air is thicker and heavier than warm air, and because of this fact gravity pulls cold air down toward the earth with more force than warm air. Also, because cold air is heavy, it can easily push the lighter warm air around.

The start of a strong wind is an area filled with air heated by the warmth of the earth. This air expands and becomes lighter and thinner. Somewhere not too far off there is usually an area where the air is colder. Often this air has been cooled by being over the cold water of the ocean. Sometimes this cold air comes from Siberia. This air, close to the ground, quickly rushes into any warm-air area, creating a wind. The cold air forces the warm air upward, where it floats on top of the heavier cold air.

To demonstrate how this happens, take a shoe box,

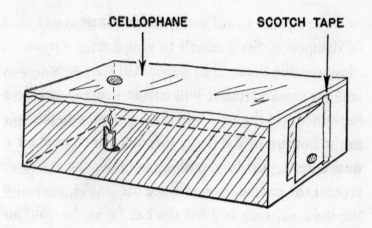

CELLOPHANE   SCOTCH TAPE

remove the cover, and cover its open top with cellophane held down by gummed tape. Cut out part of one end of the box with a knife to make a door, and hinge the door in place with tape. Cut a hole the size of a quarter near the bottom of the door, and cut a similar hole in the cellophane top of the box about two inches from the other end.

Now light a short piece of candle and put it inside the box directly beneath the hole in the roof. Close the door and seal it tight with tape. You are now creating an area of warm air.

Take a paper towel and sprinkle a little water on it to dampen it. Set a match to it and after a moment blow out the flame. The paper will start to smolder, and the smoke from it will enable you to watch the movements of the air. Hold the paper close to the hole in the bottom of the door, through which cool air is now entering the box, pushing in under the warm air around the candle. You will see the smoke, borne by the cold air, rush toward the candle as the cold air makes the wind blow.

How the Sun Draws Water into the Air

We have seen that there is always a lot of water in the air. How does it get there?

Most of it is drawn up into the air from large bodies of water on the earth, from the oceans and big lakes and rivers. The heat of the sun warms the water and this makes the molecules in the water start moving around in all directions. Billions of them whiz upward into the air, and that is how water gets into the air.

This process is called "evaporation." Evaporation takes place only where water touches air, and it takes

place faster on a hot day than on a cold one. This is because heat speeds up the motion of the molecules.

You can prove this by a very simple experiment. Fill two tin pans part full of water. Be sure the same amount of water is in each pan. Put one pan on the refrigerator or in some other cool spot, and put the other one on a radiator, on the back of a warm stove, or out in the sun. You will soon see that the water in the heated pan is evaporating, for the water will dwindle away.

How to Make a Rainstorm

Cool air causes winds, as we have just seen, and it is also one of the chief factors in making rain.

The starting point of rain is the water vapor in the air. It is invisible, but it is there all the time in large quantities. When air grows cool high up in the sky, away from the warm earth, its coolness changes the water vapor into a liquid. This liquid is in the form of tiny droplets, so small that you can't see them. But when billions of them mass together, they form clouds and become visible. Scientists have calculated that it would take about 200 million of these cloud droplets to fill a teaspoon with water!

The droplets of water in a cloud are always falling out of it, but they are usually swept away by air currents before they reach the earth. But when cool air condenses great quantities of vapor into clouds quite quickly, the clouds become very full and heavy. More and more drops of water fall out of them, and finally there are so many that the air currents can't blow them away. Then we have rain.

You can imitate Nature and make your own rain-

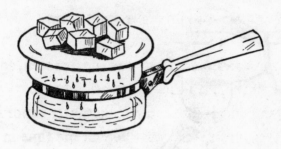

storm very easily. The equipment needed is a pyrex saucepan, a saucer, and some ice cubes. Put a cup of water in the saucepan and put it on the stove over a low flame so the water will heat slowly. This will make the air in the pan warm and will also fill it with water vapor, the raw material of rain.

When the water is warm, put the saucer on top of the pan and fill it with ice cubes. These represent the cold air of the upper atmosphere, and when the water vapor contacts the cold saucer it will be turned into a liquid. Little drops will begin to form on the bottom of the saucer. Before long they will combine to form raindrops and will fall into the pan like a miniature rainstorm.

Another Way to Make Rain

For this experiment you will need a teakettle and a glass jar. Fill the kettle half full of water and heat the water on a stove. As the water grows warm, its molecules will start to dance around and the water will start to evaporate. This will form water vapor. When the vapor leaves the spout of the kettle and cools in the air, it condenses and forms into small droplets of water. These will make a little cloud that you can see.

Now hold the jar mouth downward over the spout of the kettle and let the water vapor fill it. Little drops of water will start to form inside the jar. Since the jar is cooler than the warm air close to the kettle, the little drops will join together to make bigger drops. The jar is then just like a cloud filling up with drops of water. Pretty soon the drops will begin to fall out of the jar, and you will have your homemade rainstorm.

How to Make a Cloud

In order to make a cloud as Nature does, you will need a cold chamber. This is made from a large tin can, such as a large fruit-juice can, with a smaller can inside. Put some ice mixed with salt in the bottom of the large can. Put the small can on the ice so that its top is level with the top of the large can. Then pack ice and salt into the space between the two cans. Wrap a bath towel around the large can to keep your fingers from getting frozen.

The ice and salt will make the air inside the small can very cold, just as cold air cools the air in the upper sky. To make a cloud, breathe into the small can. The cold will instantly condense the water vapor in your breath, change it into water droplets, and form a cloud inside the can.

How to Make a Snowstorm

In this experiment you make a snowstorm by "seeding" the cloud you have made in the cold chamber. Snowflakes begin in clouds as tiny ice crystals, which form when temperatures drop below freezing. The small crystals grow larger as more moisture freezes around them, and they are finally heavy enough to fall out of the clouds as snowflakes.

A cloud must be very cold—about thirty-one degrees below zero Fahrenheit—to form ice crystals. People who make artificial rain and snow fill warmer clouds with bits of dry ice or with particles of silver iodide, around which ice crystals can form and grow.

In this experiment you use dry ice, which you can get at a drugstore. (Always handle dry ice through several thicknesses of cloth or paper to keep it from freezing your fingers.) After you have made a cloud in the cold chamber, as described in the previous experiment, scrape a few small bits off a chunk of dry ice with a nail. Let them drop into the cloud, and then shine a flashlight into the small can and watch what happens.

Thousands of tiny ice crystals will be formed very

quickly. You can see them sparkle. Breathe gently into the cloud to supply added moisture to make the crystals grow. Wait two minutes and breathe into the cloud again. Repeat this several times. This should make the crystals large and heavy enough to drop out of the cloud as very small snowflakes!

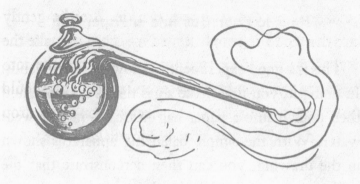

HOMEMADE GASES

THERE ARE many different kinds of gases which have interesting properties. It is not generally realized, for instance, that all gases have weight just as do solids and liquids. Some gases are lighter than air and some are very heavy. Some will burn; others won't catch fire even if you build a bonfire under them.

Most gases are made in big chemical factories or petroleum refineries, and are sold in units of about a million cubic feet at a time. The ordinary person can't get them to experiment with. For that reason, most of these experiments are done with carbon dioxide that you can easily make in your own home.

165

How to Pour Gas into a Paper Bag

This is a good experiment to show to your friends. In doing it, you first make a gas that is invisible, and then pour it into a paper bag just as though it were water. With the simple balancing apparatus shown in the drawing, you can then demonstrate that the gas you have made is heavier than air.

First make the balance by fastening two paper bags with thread to a yardstick, and then tying the yardstick to a pencil or stick held in place beneath some books placed near the edge of a table.

The gas you are going to use is carbon dioxide, and you make it by putting a spoonful of baking soda in a quart jar and then adding four tablespoonfuls of vinegar. The reaction between the soda and the vinegar will immediately form carbon dioxide. Pick up the jar and tilt it over one of the paper bags in order to pour the gas into the bag. Be careful not to pour out any of the vinegar.

You won't be able to see anything in the bag, but you will soon have proof that the gas is going into the bag, for it will become heavier and will drop toward the ground, tilting the balance as it does so.

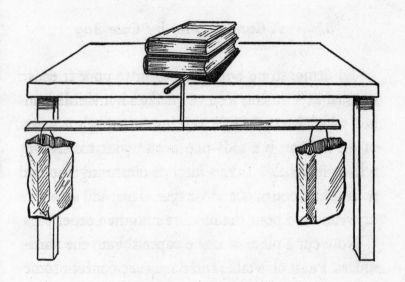

How to Make Gas from a Candle
Manufacture Water

When the gas hydrogen is burned, it unites with oxygen drawn from the air. One result of this is that the hydrogen and oxygen unite in the proper proportions to form water.

You can demonstrate this by chilling a spoon in the icebox and then holding it beside a candle flame. The water formed by the hydrogen and oxygen will gather in small drops on the spoon. It condenses on the spoon because it is cold.

A Cannon Shot by Gas

To demonstrate how gas expands you can do an unusual experiment. You can make a homemade cannon which has carbon dioxide inside it. The main part of the cannon is a soda-pop bottle with a cork that will fit it tightly. Take a kitchen measuring cup and pour into it one ounce of vinegar. Then add an ounce of water, and pour the mixture into the bottle.

Now cut a piece of tissue paper about four inches square. Put it on a table and put a teaspoonful of baking soda (sodium bicarbonate) on it. Then roll up the paper to make a little tube and twist the ends to keep the soda from falling out.

Take the bottle outside so no damage will be done to anything in the house. Put the tissue paper containing the soda into the bottle, and insert the cork. Then stand by and watch the proceedings.

The vinegar and water will soon wet the tissue paper and contact the baking soda. The mixture will form carbon dioxide, which will gradually fill the bottle and build up pressure inside it. When the pressure gets strong enough, it will force out the cork, which will shoot out of the bottle with a loud pop.

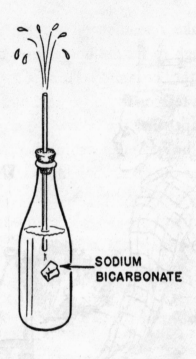

SODIUM
BICARBONATE

How to Make a Gas-operated Fountain

You should do this exciting experiment out-of-doors so the fountain won't damage anything in the house.

You will need a pop bottle, a rubber stopper with a hole in it, and an eighteen-inch piece of glass or plastic tubing open at each end. Put the tube through the hole in the stopper and keep it handy.

Next, make a solution of half vinegar and half water—enough to fill the bottle three-quarters full. Pour it into the bottle and make a tissue-paper packet containing a teaspoonful of sodium bicarbonate. Put the tissue paper into the bottle. Then put the cork and tube in the bottle and watch what happens.

As soon as the materials start to form carbon dioxide, the pressure of the gas against the top of the liquid will force it up through the tube and high into the air like the jet of a fountain.

How to Draw Off Gases from a Candle

A candle flame is a miniature scientific laboratory in which a number of interesting things take place. One of these is the production of gases. In the center of the flame the paraffin of the candle is turned into gases by the heat of the outside part of the flame. The principal gases are hydrogen and carbon dioxide.

By drawing off these gases and burning them, you can demonstrate their presence. To do this, twist a piece of wire around a glass medicine dropper from which the bulb has been removed, and hold the wide end of the dropper in the center of a candle flame. The gases will then pass upward through the dropper and you can ignite them with a match as they pass out through the small end of the dropper.

If you allowed these gases to stay in the candle flame they would be burned up.

A Gas-propelled "Perpetual Motion" Machine

You can do a very amusing and interesting experiment by using carbon dioxide to make moth balls move up and down in a glass of water. The moth balls will rise and fall for an hour or more, or long enough to justify calling their movement "perpetual motion."

The carbon dioxide that you use for this experiment is contained in a bottle of soda water, which you can get at a drugstore or grocery store. Soda water is made by charging water with carbon dioxide, and the bubbles you see in it are made by carbon dioxide as it escapes from the water.

To do the experiment, fill a glass half full of water and drop three or four moth balls into it. The moth balls will sink to the bottom, since each one is heavier

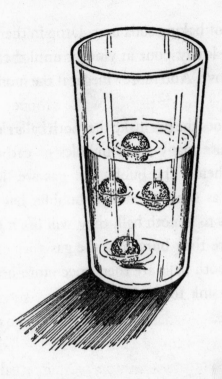

than an equal volume of water. Then slowly pour soda water into the glass, watching the moth balls as you do so. When they begin to rise, stop pouring. But if they then fall to the bottom and stay there, add a little more soda. The moth balls should then move slowly up and down.

You can also do this experiment by using vinegar and baking soda to make the carbon dioxide. Fill the glass two thirds full of water and dissolve half a teaspoonful of baking soda in it. Drop in the moth balls, and then slowly pour in vinegar until the moth balls start to move. Add more vinegar if the moth balls stop moving.

Why does the gas make the moth balls rise and fall? It is because many small bubbles of carbon dioxide cling to them. The bubbles of gas are lighter than water, so as soon as enough bubbles have attached themselves to a moth ball, they will lift it to the surface. There they burst and the gas goes off into the air. The moth balls are then once more heavier than water and sink to the bottom.

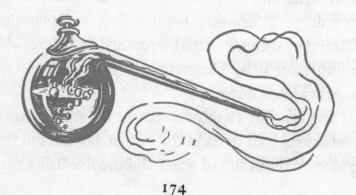

EXPERIMENTS WITH SEEDS AND PLANTS

DID YOU EVER REALIZE that we all depend for our health and strength on seeds? The plants we eat grow from seeds. Many domestic animals get their strength from seeds and plants. We in turn eat their meat in the form of roast beef and hamburger; lamb chops and mutton; ham, sausages and bacon.

Seeds are actually tiny plants surrounded by food. When air, warmth, and moisture are applied, the little plants inside seeds use the food stored with them to start their growth. They send out roots and leaves.

The roots draw in water containing minerals from the soil. The water passes up into the leaves, which absorb carbon dioxide from the air. From these materials the leaves manufacture glucose, a form of sugar, which is turned into more complex substances. By means of the green substance called chlorophyll leaves are able to use the energy of the sun and make their own food.

The experiments that follow show some of the interesting ways in which plants grow and function.

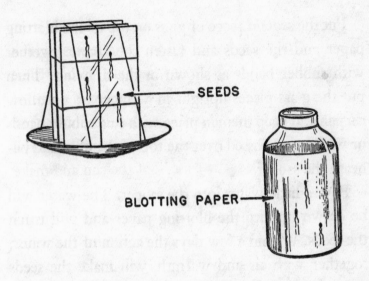

SEEDS

BLOTTING PAPER

How to Watch Seeds Sprout Roots

When you plant a seed in the earth, it is hidden and you cannot watch it send out its roots. The experiment that follows makes it possible for you to study this interesting process, which few people ever see.

Get two pieces of glass, each about four inches long and three inches wide. Then cut out a piece of blotting paper of the same size. Put the blotting paper on one of the pieces of glass and place a few small seeds on it. (Radish and grass seeds are good ones to try, but you can also use other small seeds.)

Put the second piece of glass on top of the blotting paper and the seeds and fasten the frame together with rubber bands as shown in the drawing. Then put the glass pieces upright in a saucer or a shallow tin pan and keep them in place with two rubber bands or with string passed over the top of the glass and beneath the saucer.

Pour a little water into the saucer. The water will be drawn up into the blotting paper and will reach the seeds. Within a few days the action of the water, together with air and warmth, will make the seeds start to sprout. As you will see from looking at them from time to time, they send out roots below and small stems and leaves above.

At first the seeds do not need the minerals of the earth or the carbon dioxide of the air. They use the food materials stored inside themselves. If you should want them to keep on growing, you would have to plant them in earth.

If you have difficulty finding pieces of glass to use for this experiment, you can use a glass bottle instead. Put a piece of blotting paper inside the bottle, curved to fit close to the bottle's sides. Then put the seeds between the blotting paper and the sides of the bottle.

How Heat and Cold Affect Seed Growth

Take the glass frame used in the last experiment and make another frame just like it. Put the same kind of seeds in each set. Then put one frame on a sunny window sill and another in a refrigerator.

You will soon see how much seeds depend on warmth to grow. The seeds placed in the sun will sprout much faster than those that have been kept in a cold place.

Why Roots Grow Down

When you plant a seed in the earth, the roots always grow downward, digging deeper into the earth. We are so used to this fact that we take it for granted. One reason for it is that the roots seek for the moisture hidden beneath them in the soil. It is almost as though they had an intelligence of their own that tells them what to do.

Roots will also seek water placed beneath them in a saucer. It is fascinating to see this and to watch the experiment as it proceeds.

Put a piece of blotting paper between two pieces of glass, as before. Put one seed on the blotting paper. Let the roots start to grow and then, after they have gotten nicely started, turn the glass pieces one quarter of the way around. The roots will then be horizontal instead of up and down. Wait a day or so, and watch. The roots will turn down toward the water. Again give the glass pieces a quarter turn. The roots will turn once more and grow downward.

No matter how you turn the glass pieces, the roots will always stretch out toward the life-giving water. The roots of a plant always try to reach water.

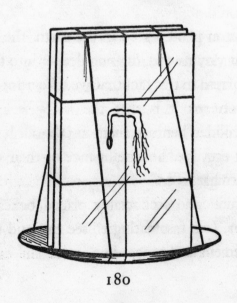

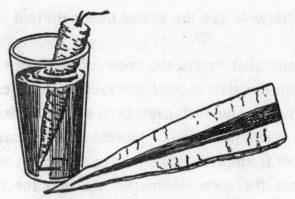

How to See the Water in a Root

As soon as a seed starts to send out roots they begin to soak up water. After a plant has grown from the seed it too keeps on absorbing water. Without water it could not live.

Did you ever see the water travel inside a root? You will if you do this experiment.

Take a fresh carrot, which is a large root, and cut off the leafy top. Then stand the carrot in a glass of water colored with red ink, red food coloring, or red Easter-egg dye. Let the carrot stay in the colored water overnight. Then slice a piece off the top with a straight knife cut, and cut the carrot in two from top to bottom. You will then be able to see where the red-colored water has traveled inside the carrot.

How to See the Water Inside a Plant

Water that enters the roots of a plant passes through the tiny ends of the roots that are called root hairs. The root hairs have surface cells that allow water to enter but prevent the water inside the root from getting out.

From the roots water rises up into the plant through sap tubes. By using colored water you can see very clearly how the sap tubes bring water to every part of a plant.

A stalk of celery is good to use for this experiment because it is white and you can easily see the colored water inside its sap tubes. Put a piece of celery in a glass of water colored red. Leave it there for three or four hours, and then examine it. You will see the red-colored water not only in the sap tubes of the stalk but also in the veins of the leaves.

A still more interesting experiment can be done by splitting a stalk of celery from the bottom about half-way to the top. Put one end of the bottom in a glass of red-colored water, and the other end in a glass of water colored blue or some other strong color. You will then be able to see the differently colored waters rise up through the sap tubes and spread through the leaf veins, coloring each half of the celery a different shade.

The same experiment can be done by using a white carnation. The whole carnation can be turned red, or one half of it can be made red while the other half remains white or is dyed some other color.

How to Demonstrate Osmosis

Plants, as we have seen, are continually taking in large amounts of water through their roots. Some of this water is used to help the plant grow. The water that is left over leaves the plant and passes off into the air.

The way in which plants draw in water through their cell walls is called osmosis. This process is one in which a thinner fluid moves through a membrane to a more dense one. It is an important process in both plant and animal life. By means of osmosis needed materials are absorbed into animal blood streams.

This experiment shows in quite a dramatic way how osmosis works to ensure a plant's water supply.

First, get a good-sized carrot. Cut off the leafy top and then hollow it out. You can use a sharp knife, but an apple corer will do a neater job.

Next, find a cork that will fit tightly into the hole in the top of the carrot and get a few soda straws from a drugstore. Get a hammer and a nail that is as thick around as a soda straw. Hold the nail and hammer it into the cork. Take out the nail

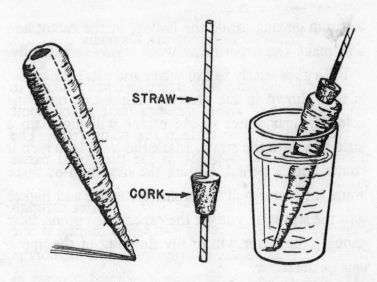

STRAW →

CORK →

and push a soda straw through the hole made by the nail.

Now fill a drinking glass one quarter full of water and add a teaspoonful of granulated sugar to the water. (This will make it denser than plain water.) Add a few drops of red or black ink to color the water. Stir the mixture until the sugar is dissolved and then pour the colored sugar water into the hole in the carrot.

Put the cork in the carrot. Then drop wax from a lighted candle all around the edges of the cork where it enters the carrot and all around the edges of the straw where it enters the cork. This will keep air from getting inside the hollow in the carrot and will make the experiment work more successfully.

Fill a glass nearly full of water and place the carrot in it as shown in the drawing. Almost at once the colored sugar water in the carrot will move up a little way into the straw. Mark the level to which it comes with a pencil. During the next two or three hours the water will move slowly higher and higher into the straw. If you let the experiment go on long enough, the water will finally flow out of the upper part of the straw.

What happens is that the water in the glass enters the cell walls of the carrot by osmosis and goes through the carrot to the hollow part, increasing the volume of water there. The excess sugar water then rises through the straw.

How to Show That Plants Give Off Water

It has already been pointed out that plants give off a great deal of water that they take in through their roots. A large tree may give off as much as fifty to a hundred gallons of water in a single day.

This is enough to fill a great many bathtubs; yet we do not see this water because it leaves the tree in the form of vapor.

You can, however, feel the effects of this water. When you walk through the woods on a warm day you will notice that the air is cooler in the woods than outside in an open field. This is because of the water that is evaporating all the time from the leaves of the trees. When water evaporates from a surface such as a tree leaf, it cools that surface.

By a simple experiment you can show how surprisingly large an amount of water a plant gives off. Get some flowers and leaves and put them in a dry drinking glass. Then cover the top of the glass with a piece of cellophane held tightly in place by a rubber band. Put the glass in the sunlight. After a few hours, the inside of the glass will be thickly covered with water droplets.

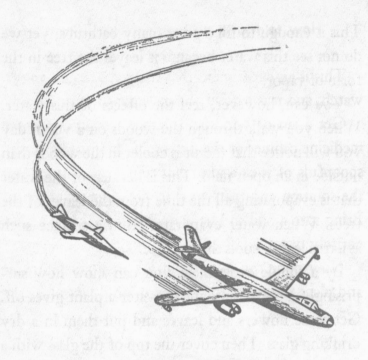

SCIENCE MAGIC

THE ASSORTED experiments in this section are quite spectacular. Most of them are especially suited to demonstrating in public. If you do them carefully, you can establish a reputation as a real scientific wizard!

How to Make a Chemical Snowstorm

This is an experiment that is always fascinating to watch, and it is a good one to show to your friends.

Get a tin of boric acid, either from your home medicine cabinet or the drugstore, and put eight teaspoonfuls of it in a glass half filled with water. Stir the solution and then pour it into a small saucepan. Bring it to a boil and let it boil until the boric acid is entirely dissolved.

Now pour the solution into a thin glass tumbler and place the tumbler in a pan of cold water. As the

solution cools, snowflakes will start to fall down through it, making a really wintry-looking snow-storm.

The cause of the storm is the fact that more boric acid can be dissolved in hot water than in cool water. As the hot solution cools, the excess boric acid solidifies and is separated from the solution, which can no longer hold it.

How to Make a Tin-Can Jet Engine

While jet propulsion is the newest thing in avia-tion, the idea on which it is based is very old. It was used as long ago as 300 A.D. by a Greek scientist named Hero in a little engine that was turned by steam coming out of jets spaced around a spherical boiler. The steam rushing out of the jets pushed back on them and made the engine spin around.

An airplane jet engine is basically a chamber that is open at just one end. Fuel is introduced into it and ignited. The burning fuel turns into hot gases which push against the closed sides and front of the chamber. This throws the gases back and out through the open

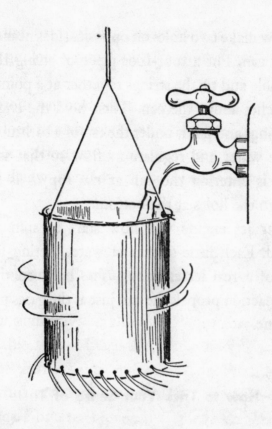

end. The plane moves forward in reaction to this
backward thrust of the jet.

To make a tin-can jet engine, cut the top of a can
off smoothly and, with a nail, punch about sixteen
evenly spaced holes in the can near the bottom. Push
the nail to the right as you make each hole so that all
the holes point at the same angle.

Now make two holes on opposite sides near the top of the can. Put a four-foot piece of string through each hole and tie the strings together at a point about ten inches above the can. Then hold the engine by the strings and put it under the tap of a bathtub. Turn on the water and regulate its flow so that as much water is entering the can at the top as is leaving through the holes at the bottom.

Your jet engine will now start to spin rapidly around. Each little stream of water, acting like the gases of a real jet engine, pushes back on the can. This reaction propels the can just as the gases propel a jet plane.

How to Trick Your Sense of Taste

Do you think your taste is all in your mouth? Well, it just isn't so! If your eyes and nose are shut tight, you can't tell the difference between a piece of apple and a piece of potato.

Here is a surprising experiment with taste to show to your friends. Ask someone, "What do you think a clean stick tastes like?" He will probably say that it doesn't taste very much like anything at all.

Give him a stick of wood and tell him to touch it to the back part of his tongue. It will taste bitter because the contact stimulates the bitter taste buds. Then tell him to touch the stick to the tip of his tongue. Here it will taste sweet because the sweet taste buds are located in that area. The stick is actually tasteless. The experiment tricks the sense of taste.

How to Exert Fifteen Thousand Pounds of Pressure with One Finger

Tell a friend that you can exert fifteen thousand pounds of pressure with one finger only, and see what he says. He will probably doubt your word or think there is a catch to it. After all, fifteen thousand pounds is seven and a half tons, and that is a lot of pressure for even a steam-hammer or a pile driver, let alone one small finger.

You can, however, easily carry out this experiment. The only equipment you need is a needle. And all you do is press the needle into a piece of cloth.

Here is the explanation: Pressure is force dis-

tributed over an area. Little forces can exert big pressures if they are working on a small surface. A force of one pound distributed over one square inch exerts a one-pound-per-square-inch pressure. Distributed over one thousandth of a square inch, the same pound will produce a pressure of a thousand pounds per square inch.

With your finger pressure you exert a force of about three quarters of a pound. When you press a needle, this force is distributed on a surface of about one twenty-thousandth of a square inch. The resulting pressure is fifteen thousand pounds per square inch.

A Spectacular Chemical Volcano

This is a very spectacular chemical experiment, but one that is absolutely safe to do. Your friends will enjoy seeing it and will probably want you to make the volcano erupt over and over again.

The chemical from which you make the volcano is ammonium bichromate. It is orange in color and you can get it at a photographic supply store or a chemical supply store. All you need for one volcano is about half a teaspoonful. Put this amount in the center of an asbestos mat (from the ten-cent store), and push the crystals into the shape of a small volcano.

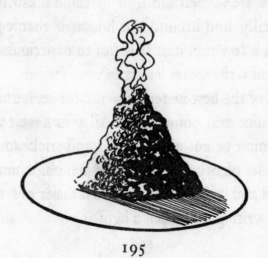

When everything is ready, turn out the lights and ignite the top of the volcano with a match. The display of fiery sparks and streams of glowing "molten lava" that follows is a reproduction in miniature of a real volcano in full eruption.

When the display is finished, you will find that the orange crystals of the ammonium bichromate have been changed by heat into a green powdery substance. This powder is green chromium oxide, which is used in coloring pottery.

How to Make Secret Inks

There are several kinds of invisible inks that you can usually find around the house or that you can make in a few minutes. It is fun to experiment with them, and write secret letters to your friends.

Two of the best materials to use for secret inks are lemon juice and onion juice. All you have to do is cut a lemon or an onion in half and stick your pen into it. Get plenty of juice on the pen point, and then go ahead and write. You will find it easier to see what you are writing if you put a light at your left side and watch the paper from the right. When the "ink" dries, it will disappear. To make the writing visible, heat the paper slowly over a candle flame or a stove.

Milk can also be used as a secret ink, and vinegar, too. But neither of these is quite as good as lemon or onion juice.

The scientific explanation of why the "ink" becomes visible is that the heat makes the ink combine with oxygen. This makes it turn dark brown, just as paper or wood becomes dark when it combines with oxygen in burning.

How to Test for Vitamin C

Vitamin C is found in citrus fruits such as oranges and lemons and in green vegetables. You can do an interesting experiment to detect it. The experiment is based on the fact that vitamin C changes iodine to a colorless liquid. In making this test, scientists usually combine iodine with starch. This makes a bright blue solution, which loses its color as vitamin C is added to it.

To do the experiment, take a cup and mix in it

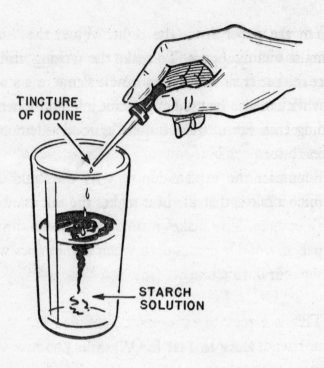

TINCTURE
OF IODINE

STARCH
SOLUTION

a spoonful of cornstarch and a little cold water to form a paste. Fill the cup with hot water and stir the paste into the water. Then boil the mixture for a few minutes and allow it to cool.

Now fill a glass half full of water. With a medicine dropper add ten drops of the cornstarch mixture. Then add one drop of tincture of iodine. This will make the solution turn almost black.

You are now ready to test a citrus juice to see if it contains vitamin C. Use orange, grapefruit, or lemon juice, either fresh or canned, and add one drop at a time with the medicine dropper. Stir the solution after adding each drop, and count the number of drops it takes to turn the blue solution to a clear liquid. You can compare the number of drops of different kinds of juice it takes to make the liquid change color.

How to Change "Ink" to "Water"

This is a science experiment that you can show your friends as a magic trick. On a table you have two glasses—one apparently empty and the other one filled with "ink." You pick up the "ink," utter the magic words, "Hey! Presto!" and pour it into the empty glass. Immediately, before everyone's eyes, the "ink" turns into clear "water"!

The chemical that does this trick for you is a bleach containing chlorine, which you can get at any grocery store. Pour a few drops of this in one of the glasses and put the glass on your table. It will appear to be empty. Fill the other glass half full of water and add enough ink to give it a deep color. Everything is then ready. All you have to do is pour the "ink" into the other glass and the magical transformation takes place.

Here is the scientific explanation: The chlorine in the bleach is very strongly attracted to hydrogen. When it is mixed with water, it immediately combines with the hydrogen in the water. This frees the oxygen in the water, which at once combines with the colored material of the ink and changes it to a colorless liquid. This also explains how bleaches remove spots from cloth. The freed oxygen combines with the spots and makes them colorless.

Be careful to keep the chlorine bleach from touching your clothing or rugs or upholstery. If it touches articles like these, it may discolor them.

How to Imitate a Hydrogen Atom

Molecules are the "building bricks" of the universe and are made up of two or more atoms. About one million different kinds of molecules or compounds have been discovered or made by man. But there are only ninety-eight different kinds of atoms known so far—one for each of the ninety-eight elements.

The simplest and most frequently found atom is the atom of hydrogen. It contains one electron, which travels in a circle around one proton. The electron is charged with negative electricity. The proton carries a charge of positive electricity. This charge of positive electricity in the proton is exactly equal to the charge of negative electricity in the electron.

Protons repel each other because they carry the same kind of electricity. Electrons also repel each other, and for the same reason. But protons and electrons attract each other. For this reason, in a hydrogen atom, the electric charges hold the electron in place as it whirls around the proton just as though there were an invisible string connecting the two.

To make a model of a hydrogen atom, get a piece of string a little over six feet long and fasten a block of wood about the size of a tennis ball to one end of it. Then take the other end of the string and whirl the wood round and round in a circle. Your hand represents the proton, the block of wood the electron, and

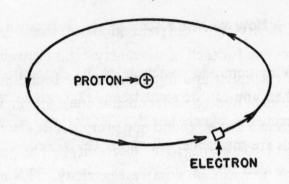

PROTON→⊕

ELECTRON

the string the electric charges that hold the electron in place as it whirls around. In a real atom, though, the electron whizzes around the proton at the rate of millions of times a second.

How to Make Laboratory Rainbows

With common materials to be found in every kitchen you can do some fascinating color-changing experiments which test for acidity and alkalinity. Acids are substances which usually have a sour taste and which turn a chemical indicator called "litmus paper" red. Alkalies neutralize acids and turn litmus paper blue. But you don't have to have litmus paper to tell whether a substance is acid or alkaline. There are other indicators which will do just as well.

Start with two or three red cabbage leaves. Cut them into shreds, cover them with rubbing alcohol, and let them stand until the alcohol has become red. Then pour the alcohol into a glass and add a little vinegar, which contains acetic acid. This will deepen the color very noticeably.

Next add a little household ammonia, which is an alkali. Pour it in slowly. The liquid is now a bright emerald green color! Your next move is to change it back to red. Do this by adding a little vinegar.

You can test various materials for acidity or alkalinity by adding them to this mixture. This solution made from red cabbage leaves is a good indicator, but so are the juices of beets, cherries, and blueberries. Try testing lemons, oranges, and grapefruits, which are acids, and soap and baking soda, which are alkalies. By using different acids and alkalies and different fruit-juice "indicators" you can make a wonderful variety of colors.

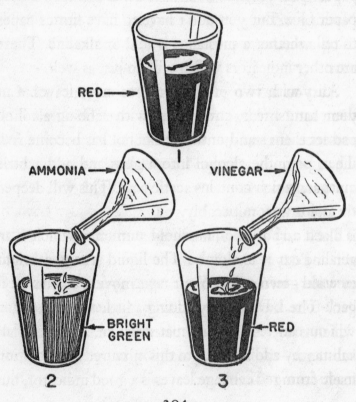

RED →

AMMONIA →   VINEGAR →

← BRIGHT GREEN   ← RED

2   3

How to Make Unburnable Sugar Burn

Hold a lighted match beneath a lump of sugar. Nothing will happen. The sugar won't ignite. But by using a scientific principle, you can make the sugar burn.

All you have to do is put some cigarette ashes in your hand and rub the lump of sugar in them. The presence of the ashes will make the sugar burn. Put the sugar on a saucer and it will keep on burning for quite some time.

The principal part of white sugar, oddly enough, is black carbon. It is combined with the gases hydrogen and oxygen in the same proportion as they occur in water—two parts of hydrogen to one part of oxygen. The burning of sugar is a chemical reaction which is not possible without the presence of another substance—the ash. Yet nothing happens to the ash itself during the process.

How to Draw Copper Out of a Penny

Pennies are not made entirely of copper, but of bronze, which is a combination of copper and tin. A penny is a pretty solid object, but in this experiment you very easily break down some of its solidity and draw out a little of the copper.

All you have to do is scrub a penny with steel wool until it is clean and shiny; then put it in a dry saucer, sprinkle a little salt on it, and just slightly moisten the salt with vinegar. The salt and vinegar will then combine with the air to work on the penny.

Leave the penny alone for about an hour, and then look at it. The salt will be colored bright green from copper that has been drawn out of the coin. The penny itself will no longer be shiny, but will be dull in color. The experiment has corroded it.

Most People Are Wrong about Airplanes

Most people believe that an airplane is supported by the air beneath it as it flies through the sky. They think it is a good deal like a ship floating on water. But the exact opposite is the truth. An airplane gets most of its "lift" from the air that flows at high speed over the top of its wings. You can easily prove this by the following experiment.

Stand a book upright on a table and put a piece of paper between its pages, as shown in the drawing. The paper represents the wing of an airplane. Put an electric fan on top of two books at one side, as shown. The fan should be placed so that its center is a little higher than the book holding the paper.

Turn on the fan and its air current will flow at high speed over the top of the paper. The book will keep most of the air from getting beneath the paper. As the air streams over the top of the "airplane wing," it will lift the paper and make it go straight out.

What actually happens is that the current of air from the fan creates a low-pressure area directly above the paper. An airplane wing is curved in such a way that the air flowing over its top surface has to travel farther and go faster than the air that passes beneath it. According to a principle discovered by the Swiss mathematician Bernoulli, when the speed of a gas or a liquid increases, the pressure decreases. You can see that this is true when you realize that the faster a gas such as air moves, the less there is of it at any given instant to exert pressure.

This explains why there is a low-pressure area above an airplane's wing—and above the piece of paper in the experiment. The air beneath the paper pushes up under it, trying to fill the low-pressure area above. The same thing happens when an airplane is in flight. The speed of the plane creates an area of reduced pressure above its wings. This is chiefly responsible for keeping it up in the air.

You can do this same experiment another way. Cut a piece of paper to make a strip about twelve inches long and two inches wide. Hold one end of the strip against your chin and blow hard. The stream of air from your breath, flowing over the upper surface of the paper, will create a low-pressure area. This will make the paper rise and stand out straight. If you did not know the principle involved, you would expect your breath to blow the paper downward.

How to Make a Geyser

You have probably seen pictures of "Old Faithful" and other geysers in Yellowstone National Park, or have visited the Park yourself and have seen the geysers erupting. It is easy to make a miniature geyser in your kitchen that will work on the same principle as the real ones.

The main part of a homemade geyser is a tin or pyrex kitchen funnel. Put the funnel in a saucepan, mouth down, and add enough water just to cover its wide tapering part. The tube will then be the only part that is above the water. Put a nail or some other small object under the rim of the funnel so the water can flow underneath it. Then put the saucepan on the stove and start to heat the water.

As the water heats and begins to turn into steam, bubbles of steam will begin to form near the bottom of the pan and beneath the funnel. They will soon start to expand and rise. The bubbles inside the funnel will push water up ahead of them, and this water will finally be pushed out of the top of the tube, making the "geyser" erupt. More water then flows into the bottom of the funnel, more bubbles are created, and

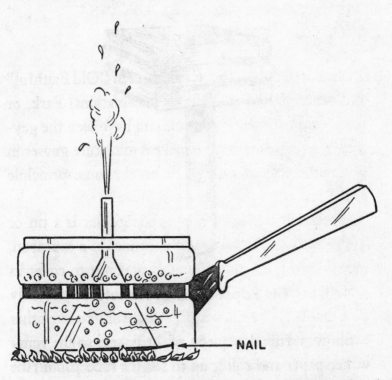

the pressure builds up again for another eruption.

A real geyser works on exactly the same principle. It is no more nor less than a spring of water deep in the earth with an opening leading to the surface of the earth. The water is warmed by heat below the earth's surface, and the water and steam are then pushed out of the top of the opening. With a geyser like "Old Faithful," the process is repeated about once every hour.

The Paper Pillar of Hercules

Show a friend a piece of ordinary white type-writer paper and roll it up to form a tube about two inches in diameter. Fasten it with a rubber band and stand the tube upright on a table.

"How strong do you think that paper is?" you ask. Your friend is pretty sure to say that it isn't very strong. Paper never is.

"Just watch, and you'll get a big surprise," you tell him.

Put a good-sized book on top of the tube. Surprisingly enough the paper will support it without buckling. Then add another book, and another and another. The tube will stand upright. Put each book carefully and gently on top of the one beneath it and keep on adding books until the tube shows signs of giving way. You will find that you can pile up five or more medium-sized books and the paper tube will support them all.

This experiment demonstrates one of the reasons why the thin steel framework of a skyscraper is able to hold up the enormous weight of the entire building. It is the form in which the framework is arranged that gives it much of its strength.

It's the Inertia That Does It

This experiment is a good stunt to show to friends. You probably have heard the fuss a steam locomotive makes when it is preparing to pull out of a station. It has to develop a good deal of power in order to overcome its inertia—its tendency to remain standing still. Another example of inertia is seen when you are sitting in an automobile and it starts forward very suddenly. What happens? You are thrown against the back of the seat—sometimes quite hard. That is because of your body's inertia.

Inertia is the propensity of every motionless body to remain where it is.

To demonstrate this property of matter, put a piece of thin cardboard on top of a drinking glass and put a penny on the card. Then quickly snap the card away by flipping your finger against it. You might think that the coin would go sailing off on the card, but it doesn't. The coin stays right where it is and drops into the glass. This makes an excellent trick when it is neatly done.

Scientific Swordsmanship

This is another surprising scientific trick that depends for its success upon the property of inertia. In doing it you instantly cut in two an apple that is suspended in mid-air.

Take a carving knife and put the edge of its blade into the top of an apple a little to one side of the stem. The blade should enter just far enough so the knife will hold the apple suspended—but not so far that your audience says you are taking an unfair advantage.

Hold the knife in your left hand with the apple in front of you and wrap a towel or a napkin around your right hand. Then strike the free end of the knife blade sharply with your right hand. The knife will cut right through the apple.

The explanation is that the property of inertia makes the apple tend to stay just where it is, and as a result of this the fast-moving knife is able to slice right through it.

NAPKIN
AROUND
HAND ↓

The Changing Handkerchief

You take a handkerchief from your pocket and show it to your friends. It looks perfectly ordinary—nothing suspicious about it at all.

"Now watch!" You hold the handkerchief over a lighted electric light bulb or a hot radiator or stove, and presto! it becomes bright blue in color. After everyone has noted the miraculous change, you breathe a magic breath on the handkerchief. The blue color disappears, and the cloth is once again white.

This is a chemical trick which is done with the aid of cobalt chloride. This can be purchased at a chemical supply house. (You can probably locate a firm of this kind in your city by asking a druggist.) Cobalt chloride is the chemical that is used to make the kind of barometer that consists of a doll with a cotton dress pasted to a piece of cardboard. The dress is impregnated with a cobalt chloride solution. When it is going to rain, the moisture in the air combines with the cobalt chloride and turns the dress a light pink. When the air is dry the cobalt chloride turns blue.

To prepare a color-changing handkerchief, simply soak it in a solution made by dropping some cobalt chloride crystals into a glass of water. This will give the handkerchief a pale pink color, but the tint is so light as to be almost colorless.

"Wine" and "Water"

This is one of the best of all the chemical magic tricks. You can get the chemicals you need for it from any drugstore.

Ask your druggist to make a solution of one gram

of phenolphthalein (FEE-nohl-THAL-een) in fifty milliliters of ethyl alcohol. This solution plus some ordinary household ammonia and vinegar is all you need.

Before you plan to show the trick to your friends, prepare your equipment. Get four small glasses and a water pitcher made of dark glass, china, or pottery. With a medicine dropper put ten drops of the solution in the first glass. Leave the second glass empty. Put ten drops of the solution in the third glass. Then put fifteen drops of vinegar in the fourth glass.

Put twelve ounces of water in the pitcher and drop into it three drops of ammonia. Stir the mixture. Now you are ready to call in your friends and show them some very surprising magic.

You begin by filling each glass with the clear water-and-ammonia mixture in the pitcher. The first glass will appear to be miraculously full of red "wine." The second glass will seem to contain clear "water." The third glass will contain "wine," and the fourth will appear to contain clear "water."

Now comes the second part of the trick. Pick up the first three glasses one by one and pour their contents back into the pitcher. Then fill these three glasses again, pouring into them the mixture contained in the pitcher. The three glasses will be filled with sparkling red "wine."

Now pick up all four glasses one by one and pour their contents into the pitcher. Fill the four glasses from the pitcher. This time there will be no "wine" at all. All the glasses will be filled with clear "water."

The scientific explanation of the trick is that the phenolphthalein-and-alcohol solution is what chemists call an "indicator." When an alkali such as ammonia is added, it turns the indicator red. When the alkali is neutralized by adding an acid (vinegar), the red solution loses its color.

The Steel Handkerchief

Show a friend an ordinary handkerchief and tell him that it has some very remarkable properties. For example, you say, you can arrange it so the handkerchief won't let water pass through it.

Fill a glass nearly full of water. Then wet the handkerchief thoroughly and put it over the top of the glass. Pull the cloth down tight and make sure that it is touching the rim of the glass all the way round. Then turn the glass upside down. You would expect the water to pass right through the cloth. But instead it stays in the glass, held in place by the "steel handkerchief."

The scientific explanation is that air pressure pushes up against the handkerchief and at the same time surface tension keeps the water from passing through the handkerchief.

Strong-Man Stunt

This is a stunt to try out on some athletic friend who is proud of his muscles and his great strength.

You prepare for it by getting a fairly heavy book and tying around it a piece of strong twine or cord about four feet long. Then you give the ends of the cord to your friend, telling him to hold one end in each hand. Ask him to extend his arms to right and left and see if he can pull the book upward until the cord is in a straight line.

You can tell your friend in advance that he will probably find it impossible to straighten out the cord. This is because it actually *is* scientifically impossible for him to do so. He may be as strong as Hercules, but that won't help him. He is battling against a scientific principle that he simply can't beat.

The principle is this: The smaller the angle between the left- and right-hand halves of the cord, the greater the force that must be exerted to hold up the book. Furthermore, if enough force could be expended to bring the cord up to a straight line, it would be so great that the cord would break under the tremendous strain. So, even if your friend were strong enough to stretch out the cord into an almost straight line, he could not achieve final success because he would break the cord.

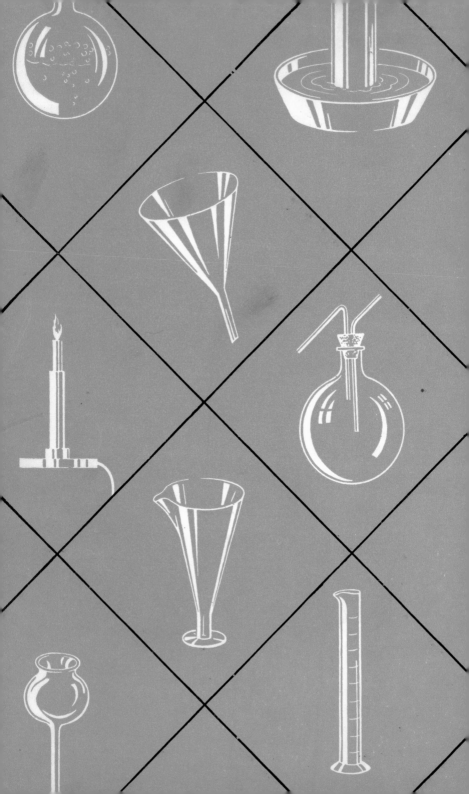